HIGHWAY
66

A UNIQUE JOURNEY THROUGH
THE 66 BOOKS OF THE BIBLE

JEFF LASSEIGNE

HIGHWAY 66
A UNIQUE JOURNEY THROUGH THE 66 BOOKS OF THE BIBLE

www.harvest.org

FOREWORD

It is my privilege to endorse my friend and colleague, Jeff Lasseigne. Jeff is the Assistant Pastor at Harvest Christian Fellowship. He is a fantastic communicator of the Word of God, and whenever I hear him speak, I am blessed and built up in my faith.

In this book, *Highway 66*, Jeff has taken a "big picture" look at the entire Bible. How important it is for us as believers to go through the whole Book, as it is all "inspired by God." In doing so, we will discover the "whole counsel of God."

You will find this series informative, and at the same time, very understandable. So buckle your seatbelts, and get on *Highway 66*!

Greg Laurie, Senior Pastor
Harvest Christian Fellowship
Riverside, California

CONTENTS

SPECIAL THANKS

TO THE FOLLOWING PEOPLE, I EXTEND MY SINCERE APPRECIATION FOR THEIR INVALUABLE ASSISTANCE IN HELPING TO BRING THIS BOOK TOGETHER: PASTOR GREG LAURIE, PASTOR PAUL EATON, DIANE JACKSON, BRIAN JACKSON, KAREN ZAPICO, MICHAEL BERGER, AND JULIE MEREDITH.

INTRODUCTION

From the moment that I committed my life to Christ in 1980, I've had a strong appetite for God's Word. I love to read it, study it, apply it, and teach it. Like the psalmist, I can say, "I rejoice at Your word as one who finds great treasure" (Psalm 119:162). Along with all the great truths and promises of Scripture, I love the nuggets—those little morsels of insight and information gleaned from the pages of God's Word. It is along those lines that I compiled the information and insights contained in this book. Highway 66 takes you on a journey through all the books of the Bible, offering you information, facts, quotes, notes, and connections to Christ.

My goal is to help us see the unique features of all 66 different books, as we deepen our understanding and appreciation of Scripture as a whole. Along with that, Highway 66 can be used as a Bible study tool for those who teach God's Word. My prayer is that it might inspire you to dig deeper in your own studies and devotions. In the words of John William Burgon, "The Bible is none other than the voice of Him that sits upon the throne. Every book of it, every chapter of it, every syllable of it, every letter of it, is the direct utterance of the Most High."

Jeff Lasseigne
Riverside, CA
January 2014

GENESIS

IMPORTANT INFORMATION

AUTHOR: **Moses**

THEME: **Origins—Man's Sin and God's Salvation**

CATEGORY: **Pentateuch**

FASCINATING FACTS

1. Genesis tells us about the beginning of everything (life, sin, salvation, judgment, marriage, family, government, etc.), except God Himself.

2. Genesis records the life of Enoch, one of only two people in the Bible who did not physically die (Elijah is the other).

3. Genesis contains the record of seven men who all lived to be over nine hundred years old (5:5, 8, 11, 14, 20, 27; 9:29).

4. Genesis tells us about the longest life on record: 969 years (Methuselah, 5:27).

5.	Genesis records the first death and murder, that of Abel (4:8).

6.	Genesis covers a longer time period (2,350) than any other book in the Bible, which is longer than the rest of the books of the Bible put together.

7.	Genesis lays out the basic foundation for all of the great doctrines of Scripture.

8.	Genesis opens with a garden and closes with a grave; it begins with creation and closes with a coffin.

9.	Genesis records the only instance in Scripture in which God rested (Genesis 2:2; also quoted in Exodus 20; 31; and Hebrews 4).

10.	Genesis records the first appearance of Satan in human history (Genesis 3:1).

11.	One-half of the great heroes of faith listed in Hebrews 11 lived during the time of Genesis.

12.	Genesis gives us the first reference to the gospel of Jesus Christ (3:15).

QUOTABLE QUOTES

"The narrative is so simple, so much like truth, so consistent everywhere within itself, so correct in its dates, so impartial in its biography, so accurate in its philosophical details, so pure in its morality, and so benevolent in its design, as amply to demonstrate that it never could have had an earthly origin."
Adam Clarke

"The book of Genesis is probably the most important book ever written...If the Bible were somehow expurgated of the book of Genesis (as many people today would prefer), the rest of the Bible would be incomprehensible. It would be like a building without a ground floor, or a bridge with no support."
Henry M. Morris

"Every single Biblical doctrine of theology, directly or indirectly, ultimately has its basis in the book of Genesis."
Ken Ham

NOTABLE NOTES

Genesis 3 is one of "the three great third chapters" of the Bible. The other two are John 3 and Romans 3. All three of these "third chapters" speak of the "three Rs": ruin, redemption, and regeneration.

CHRIST CONNECTIONS

Christ can be found in Genesis as:
Creator
Seed of the Woman
Ark of Salvation

EXODUS

IMPORTANT INFORMATION

AUTHOR: **Moses**

THEME: **Redemption, Deliverance**

CATEGORY: **Pentateuch**

FASCINATING FACTS

1. In Exodus, we see the birth of the nation of Israel.

2. In Exodus, we have the beginning of Israel's Passover and its subsequent observation (chapter 12).

3. In Exodus, we also see the beginning of the Tabernacle, the priesthood, and the yearly festivals.

4. Exodus gives us the beginning of the Law, highlighted by the Ten Commandments.

5. Exodus gives us the clearest picture of God's salvation in the Old Testament.

6. In Exodus, there are perhaps more symbols of Christ than in any other Old Testament book, such as: Moses, the Passover Lamb, the Tabernacle, and the Ark.

7. Eleven chapters of Exodus (more than one-quarter of the book) are devoted to the instructions about the Tabernacle.

8. In Exodus, we see many miracles and miraculous events, highlighted by the parting of the Red Sea.

9. Exodus presents a contrast in tens: ten plagues and Ten Commandments.

10. The ten plagues in Exodus, performed by God through Moses served as a challenge to numerous false gods of Egypt.

11. In this book, Moses led the exodus from Egypt and was a type of Christ; in the Gospels, Jesus spoke of His exodus on the Mount of Transfiguration and Moses appeared next to Him (Luke 9:31).

12. Exodus records the first great praise songs in the Bible (chapter 15), led by Moses and his sister Miriam.

QUOTABLE QUOTES

"Exodus stands at the heart of the Old Testament as the greatest example of the saving acts of God before Christ."
Talk Thru the Bible

"It took one night to take Israel out of Egypt, but forty years to take Egypt out of Israel."
George H. Morrison

"The life of Moses presents a series of antitheses. He was the child of a slave, and the son of a queen. He was born in a hut, and lived in a palace. He inherited poverty, and

he lived in royalty. He was the leader of armies, and the keeper of flocks. He was the mightiest of warriors, and the meekest of men. He was educated in the court, and dwelt in the desert. He had the wisdom of Egypt, and the faith of a child. He was fitted for the city, and wandered in the wilderness. He was tempted with the pleasures of sin, and endured the hardship of virtue. He was backward in speech, and talked with God. He had the rod of a shepherd, and the power of the Infinite. He was a fugitive from Pharaoh, and an ambassador from heaven. He was the giver of the Law, and the forerunner of grace. He died alone on Mount Nebo, and appeared with Christ on the Mount of Transfiguration. No man assisted at his funeral, yet God buried him."
H. I. Haldeman

NOTABLE NOTES

In the book of Revelation, chapter 15, reference is made to the saints in heaven singing the "Song of Moses" for their deliverance and victory. That song, which is recorded in Exodus 15, supplies the lyrics to a song that God's people will sing together in heaven.

CHRIST CONNECTIONS

Christ can be found in Exodus as:
Passover Lamb
Deliverer
High Priest

LEVITICUS

IMPORTANT INFORMATION

AUTHOR: **Moses**

THEME: **Holiness, Worship, Communion**

CATEGORY: **Pentateuch**

FASCINATING FACTS

1. No other book in the Bible contains so many direct messages from God as Leviticus does (1:1; 4:1; 11:44; etc.).

2. Leviticus speaks more about holiness than any other book of the Bible.

3. It is the first of only three books in Scripture that begins by stating that God is speaking (see also: Numbers, Joshua).

4. In Leviticus, the Holy Spirit is never mentioned by name, though all of the other books of the Pentateuch refer to Him.

5. The New Testament quotes or refers to Leviticus more than 100 times.

6. The words "holy," "blood," "priest," and "sacrifice" appear more times in Leviticus than in any other book of the Bible.

7. Leviticus covers a time period of only one month (Exodus 40:17, Numbers 1:1), and records no geographical movement in the history of Israel.

8. Even though the title "Leviticus" means "pertaining to the Levites," there is only one casual mention of the Levites in this book (25:32).

9. Levi, from whom the Levites descended, was the third son of Jacob and the great grandfather of Aaron, Moses, and Miriam.

10. In chapters 11–15 alone, the word "unclean" appears more than 100 times.

11. The two main symbols of evil in Scripture are referred to in this book: leprosy and leaven.

QUOTABLE QUOTES

"Holiness is the Grand Theme of the book of Leviticus. A Holy God is seen providing a Holy Savior who through the power of the Holy Spirit enables the believer to worship God in the Beauty of Holiness."
W. G. Heslop

"Leviticus stands in the same relation to Exodus that the Epistles do to the Gospels."
C. I. Scofield

"Considering that it embraces the history of only one month, this may claim to be the most remarkable book in the Old Testament."
Joseph Parker

"The holiness of God shines like a white, fearful light upon the whole book."
G. Campbell Morgan

NOTABLE NOTES

In Leviticus 23, Moses makes mention of the three great feast days: Passover, Pentecost, and Tabernacles. Passover reminds us of Jesus Christ, our Passover Lamb, whose blood cleanses us from sin; Pentecost reminds us of the Holy Spirit being poured out upon believers at Pentecost, when the Church was born; and Tabernacles reminds us of the Father and how He provided for and protected His people in the wilderness. Therefore, in these three great feasts, we see a picture of the Trinity: Father, Son, and Holy Spirit.

CHRIST CONNECTIONS

Christ can be found in Leviticus as:
High Priest
Sacrifice

NUMBERS

IMPORTANT INFORMATION

AUTHOR: **Moses**

THEME: **Our Service and Walk; Consequences of Unbelief**

CATEGORY: **Pentateuch**

FASCINATING FACTS

1. Several of the events described in Numbers are used in the New Testament to warn believers about the consequences of sin and unbelief (1 Corinthians 10; 1 Peter 2; Jude; etc.).

2. The sin of Balaam (chapters 22–25) is mentioned by three different New Testament writers in their books: Peter, Jude, and John.

3. It is the second of only three books in Scripture that begins by stating that God is speaking (see also: Leviticus, Joshua).

4. It is the first book of the Bible to record a detailed census (chapters 1, 26).

5.   The word "wilderness" is used forty-five times in this book.

6.   The raising up of the brass serpent in Numbers 21 is one of the clearest Old Testament pictures of Jesus hanging on the cross, and of people being saved by faith (John 3:14).

7.   Numbers records several instances of rebellion against God's ordained leadership (14:2; 16:2; 16:41; 20:2; 21:4).

8.   Numbers records God's selection of Joshua to succeed Moses (27:18–23) and to lead the people into the Promised Land.

9.   Numbers explains the Nazirite Vow (chapter 6), the Red Heifer sacrifice (chapter 19), and the institution of the six Cities of Refuge (chapter 35).

10. Numbers 20 records the deaths of both Miriam and Aaron.

QUOTABLE QUOTES

"The faithfulness of God is clearly seen in the fact that three million men, women, and children enter into, and pass through, a sterile desert without a drop of water, a loaf of bread, or a blade of grass! An army of three million men, women, and children enter into and pass through a trackless, pathless, uncharted desert without a guide, compass, chart, map, footstep, finger post, or stop and go sign … without a grocery store, bakery, meat market, surgeon, doctor, butcher, undertaker, drug store, or hospital. Think about the faithfulness of God."
W. G. Heslop

"The story of Numbers is of deep interest … every careful reader of the New Testament Scriptures knows that Numbers" is there repeatedly quoted.   **Arno C. Gaebelein**

"[Numbers] is a story at once depressing and inspiring; according as we look at the shameful unbelief of man, or at the unfailing love of God...There is no royal road into blessing; where the people of God fall they must rise; where they deny they must confess, and to the point from which they wander from God must they return; blessing can be found only where it was lost. This, in the main, is the subject of Numbers."
W. Graham Scroggie

NOTABLE NOTES

In Numbers 20, Miriam dies, Moses loses his entry into the Promised Land, and Aaron dies. The Law (Moses), the Priesthood (Aaron), and Prophecy (Miriam) could not bring us into the Promised Land, but Jesus (Joshua) could!

CHRIST CONNECTIONS

Christ can be found in Numbers as:
Pillar of Cloud/Fire
Tabernacle
Smitten Rock
Star Out of Jacob

DEUTERONOMY

Dear Friend,

We would like to apologize for an error found on pages 13–14 of this edition of Highway 66. The "Fascinating Facts" section of Deuteronomy contains information from the book of Joshua.

Below, you can find the correct information for this section. Again, we are sorry for any inconvenience this may have caused.

Harvest Ministries

IMPORTANT INFORMATION

AUTHOR: Moses

THEME: Obedience to God; God's Love for His People

CATEGORY: Pentateuch

FASCINATING FACTS

1. Deuteronomy contains the longest recorded farewell speech in the Bible, given by Moses in chapters 31–33.

2. Jesus quoted from Deuteronomy three times in the wilderness to defeat Satan's temptations (Matthew 4:1–11), and also to sum up the Law (Matthew 22:37).

3. Deuteronomy 33:16 contains the only Old Testament reference to God in the burning bush (Exodus 3).

4. Deuteronomy is quoted or alluded to more than ninety-five times in seventeen different books of the New Testament.

5. Deuteronomy makes the first mention of death by hanging on a tree (21:22–23).

6. Deuteronomy has been nicknamed "The Gospel of Love," and the word "love" is used some twenty-one times in this book.

7. Deuteronomy makes at least 250 references to its four preceding books, and is referred to itself over 350 times in the rest of the Old Testament.

8. Moses is the only person in Scripture who is said to have been buried by God Himself (34:6).

9. This book contains the great prediction of the coming Prophet (Messiah/Christ) in Deuteronomy 18:15–19.

10. Of all of the books of the Pentateuch, the prophets most used and quoted from Deuteronomy in their books.

11. Moses repeats the phrase "the Lord your God" to the people more than 250 times in Deuteronomy.

12. Jesus quoted more from the book of Deuteronomy than from any other book of the Pentateuch.

QUOTABLE QUOTES

"The book of Deuteronomy is the book which demands obedience. Obedience is the keynote of almost every chapter. It is the great lesson of the book. Obedience in the spirit of love, flowing from a blessed and enjoyed relationship with Jehovah, is the demand made of His people."
Arno C. Gaebelein

"It may be safely asserted that very few parts of the Old Testament Scriptures can be read with greater profit by the genuine Christian than the book of Deuteronomy." **Adam Clarke**

DEUTERONOMY

IMPORTANT INFORMATION

AUTHOR: **Moses**

THEME: **Obedience to God; God's Love for His People**

CATEGORY: **Pentateuch**

FASCINATING FACTS

1. The name of Moses appears fifty-seven times in the book of Joshua, showing that even though Moses had died, his words and works had not been forgotten. The book of Joshua begins and ends with death (1:1; 24:33).

2. The message of Joshua is to the Old Testament what the message of Ephesians is to the New Testament: possessing our inheritance.

3. In Joshua 6:26, a remarkable threefold prophecy is made about the city of Jericho, which was fulfilled some five hundred years later (1 Kings 16:34).

4. The great event in Moses' life was the passage through the Red Sea, and the great event in Joshua's life was the passage through the Jordan River.

5. In Joshua, we read of four incredible miracles that took place: the crossing of the Jordan, the fall of Jericho, the "selective" hailstones, and the sun standing still.

6. Rahab, whose story is recorded in chapters 2 and 6, is the first known Gentile who was converted under Mosaic Law.

7. The word "land" is used over eighty-five times in this book, while the words "inheritance" and "inherit" appear over sixty times, emphasizing Israel's possession of the Promised Land.

8. Joshua refers to nine memorials of stones or altars to commemorate important events.

9. Joshua is the third of only three books in Scripture that begin by stating that God is speaking (see also: Leviticus, Numbers).

10. Joshua is the first book of the Bible named after its main character.

11. Joshua records one of the best-known and best-loved Bible stories: the fall of Jericho.

QUOTABLE QUOTES

"The book of Deuteronomy is the book which demands obedience. Obedience is the keynote of almost every chapter. It is the great lesson of the book. Obedience in the spirit of love, flowing from a blessed and enjoyed relationship with Jehovah, is the demand made of His people."
Arno C. Gaebelein

"It may be safely asserted that very few parts of the Old Testament Scriptures can be read with greater profit by the genuine Christian than the book of Deuteronomy." **Adam Clarke**

"Moses, at the close of his life, looked upon a new generation, a new land, a new life, a new leader, and so there was the need for this new revelation of the Divine 'love,' nowhere mentioned until now, though much illustrated...It is probably true that Deuteronomy is the most spiritual Book in the Old Testament."
W. Graham Scroggie

NOTABLE NOTES

According to Deuteronomy 34, Moses died just outside the Promised Land and was not allowed to enter in. However, Moses did eventually make it in. Later on, in the Gospels, Moses is seen inside of the Promised Land on the Mount of Transfiguration, talking with Jesus and Elijah! (Matthew 17:3; Luke 9:30–31)

CHRIST CONNECTIONS

Christ can be found in Deuteronomy as:
Prophet like Moses
Law Giver

JOSHUA

IMPORTANT INFORMATION

AUTHOR: **Joshua**

THEME: **Possessing Our Inheritance**

CATEGORY: **History**

FASCINATING FACTS

1. The name of Moses appears fifty-seven times in the book of Joshua, showing that even though Moses had died, his words and works had not been forgotten.

2. The book of Joshua begins and ends with death (1:1; 24:33).

3. The message of Joshua is to the Old Testament what the message of Ephesians is to the New Testament: possessing our inheritance.

4. In Joshua 6:26, a remarkable threefold prophecy is made about the city of Jericho, which was fulfilled some five hundred years later (1 Kings 16:34).

5. The great event in Moses' life was the passage through the Red Sea, and the great event in Joshua's life was the passage through the Jordan River.

6. In Joshua, we read of four incredible miracles that took place: the crossing of the Jordan, the fall of Jericho, the "selective" hailstones, and the sun standing still.

7. Rahab, whose story is recorded in chapters 2 and 6, is the first known Gentile who was converted under Mosaic Law.

8. The word "land" is used over eighty-five times in this book, while the words "inheritance" and "inherit" appear over sixty times, emphasizing Israel's possession of the Promised Land.

9. Joshua refers to nine memorials of stones or altars to commemorate important events.

10. Joshua is the third of only three books in Scripture that begin by stating that God is speaking (see also: Leviticus, Numbers).

11. Joshua is the first book of the Bible named after its main character.

12. Joshua records one of the best-known and best-loved Bible stories: the fall of Jericho.

QUOTABLE QUOTES

"The book of Joshua records one of the most interesting and important portions of Israel's history. It is the capstone to the books of Moses, the foundation of those which follow. Omit Joshua, and there is a gap left in the sacred history which nothing could supply."
A. W. Pink

"As I have studied Joshua, I have become convinced that this is a message very much needed in our time. We have many professing Christians in our day...but we do not seem to have many Joshuas. We do not have many who, without trying to be novel or spectacular, determine to obey the law of God in every particular and then actually do obey it throughout a lifetime of faithful service."
James Montgomery Boice

"I think the church needs the message of the book of Joshua more than ever before...The book of Joshua tells us how to be victorious soldiers and how to claim our rich spiritual inheritance in Jesus Christ. It tells us how to be strong and courageous as we face our enemies and march forward to claim new territory for the Lord."
Warren W. Wiersbe

NOTABLE NOTES

Rahab, the prostitute turned convert (chapter 2), has several special distinctions in Scripture: hers was the first recorded conversion of a woman in the Bible; she is one of only four women referred to by name in the genealogy of Jesus (see Matthew 1); and she is one of only two women mentioned by name in Hebrews 11, the great "Hall of Faith."

CHRIST CONNECTIONS

Christ can be found in Joshua as:
Captain of Our Salvation
Victorious Leader

JUDGES

IMPORTANT INFORMATION

AUTHOR: **Unknown**

THEME: **Israel's Compromise and God's Compassion**

CATEGORY: **History**

FASCINATING FACTS

1. Judges is one of four Old Testament books with an unknown author (see also: Ruth, Esther, and Job).

2. The time of Judges has been called "the Dark Ages" of Israel's history.

3. Judges contains the oldest known parable in the world (9:8–15).

4. Judges contains the record of the first female leader of Israel: Deborah (chapter 4).

5. Judges records one of the worst stories of depravity found in Scripture (chapters 19–21).

6. Judges tells the story of thirteen different "judges" or

"deliverers," four of whom are listed in the "Hall of Faith" in Hebrews 11:32.

7. In Judges, various forms of the word "deliver" occur some forty-eight times.

8. Judges contains one-fourth of the Old Testament references to the "Angel of the Lord," who is undoubtedly Christ Himself.

9. Judges tells of the strongest man recorded in history: Samson.

10. Judges tells of the first Nazirite recorded in history: Samson.

11. Judges contains the first two recorded suicides in Scripture: Abimelech, Gideon's son (9:54); and Samson (16:30).

12. Judges records the only instance in Scripture in which someone is called "a very fat man" (3:17, Eglon).

QUOTABLE QUOTES

"As we cannot obliterate the tragic record [of Judges], let us be quick to learn from it; for although it is such a pathetic anticlimax to the book of Joshua, it is nevertheless one of the richest books in Scripture in the salutary lessons and examples which it contains."
J. Sidlow Baxter

"The book of Judges is perhaps less studied and quoted from than most other historical books of Scripture... but even the most neglected parts of the Lord's garden will be found to yield flowers of heavenly fragrance."
Luke H. Wiseman

"Judges, more than any other book of the Bible, illustrates the way God works through ordinary people to accomplish His purposes."
Cyril J. Barber

NOTABLE NOTES

This seventh book of the Bible records seven distinct cycles, which include: seven apostasies of Israel, their seven subjections to seven heathen nations, seven pleas for rescue to God, and seven deliverances.

CHRIST CONNECTIONS

Christ can be found in Judges as:
Judge and Law Giver
Deliverer

RUTH

IMPORTANT INFORMATION

AUTHOR: Unknown

THEME: God's Plan of Redemption

CATEGORY: History

FASCINATING FACTS

1. The book of Ruth is the only instance in Scripture in which an entire book is devoted to the history of one woman.

2. Ruth is the second of four Old Testament books with an unknown author (see also: Judges, Esther, and Job).

3. Ruth is the first of only two books in the Bible named after a woman (see also: Esther).

4. Ruth is one of only four women referred to by name in the genealogy of Jesus, as recorded in Matthew 1.

5. Ruth contains the second recorded conversion of a Gentile in Scripture (the first was Rahab's; see Joshua 2).

6. The book of Ruth gives us an illustration of the family marriage duty/custom of that day (Deuteronomy 25:5–10).

7. The book of Ruth begins with a series of funerals and ends with a wedding. It opens with a famine and closes with a family.

8. The name of David is mentioned for the first time in Scripture, in Ruth 4:17.

9. The Hebrew word *ga'al*, translated "redeem" and "redeemer," is found thirteen times in this book.

10. The book of Ruth is read annually by orthodox Jews on the Feast of Pentecost, because Ruth's betrothal took place during harvest season when Pentecost is observed.

QUOTABLE QUOTES

"After reading Judges … Ruth is like a lily in a stagnant pond. Here, instead of unfaithfulness, is loyalty; and instead of immorality, is purity. Here, instead of battlefields are harvest fields, and instead of the warrior's shout is the harvester's song."
W. Graham Scroggie

"What Venus is to statuary and the Mona Lisa is to paintings, Ruth is to literature."
John F. MacArthur Jr.

"It seems incredible that this beautiful love story could occur during the dark days of the judges, but such is the grace of God. We are living in trying days today; yet God is at work in His world, getting a bride for His Son and accomplishing His eternal purposes. Never permit the bad news of man's sin to rob you of the good news of God's love and grace."
-Warren W. Wiersbe

NOTABLE NOTES

Dr. Samuel Johnson, the great literary authority of the eighteenth century, once read the story of Ruth to his friends in a London club. After he had finished reading it, his listeners thought it had just recently been written, and they were loud in their praises for its simple beauty. Dr. Johnson then informed his listeners, to their surprise, that he had just read the book of Ruth, taken from the book that they all despised: the Bible!

CHRIST CONNECTIONS

Christ can be found in Ruth as:
Kinsman Redeemer
Lover
Protector

1 SAMUEL

IMPORTANT INFORMATION

AUTHOR: **Samuel, Nathan, and Gad**

THEME: **The Establishing of the Kingdom of Israel**

CATEGORY: **History**

FASCINATING FACTS

1. 1 Samuel records the name of God as "Lord of Hosts" for the first time in Scripture (1:3). It is the first of 281 Old Testament occurrences.

2. 1 Samuel contains two of seven suicides recorded in Scripture, and the only back-to-back suicides (31:4–5).

3. Samuel was the last judge of the 350-year period of the Judges.

4. Samuel anointed Israel's first two kings: Saul (10:1) and David (16:13).

5. Samuel is the first biblical book to use the word "anointed" (2:10), which is the origin of the word "Messiah."

6. Samuel gives us the original title by which the prophets were known: "Seer," meaning "to see" (9:9).

7. 1 Samuel contains the first mention of a school of prophets, which most believe was founded by Samuel (10:5; 19:20).

8. 1 Samuel opens up with the birth of Samuel, Israel's last judge, and closes with the death of Saul, Israel's first king.

9. 1 Samuel contains the only biblical references of the ill-fated name "Ichabod," which means "Where is the glory?" (4:21; 14:3).

10. The word "prayer" is used over thirty times in this book.

11. One of the greatest examples of friendship found anywhere in Scripture is recorded in 1 Samuel 18: David and Jonathan.

12. 1 Samuel describes the largest man found in Scripture, Goliath, who was at least nine feet nine inches tall (17:4)!

QUOTABLE QUOTES

"It is astonishing how full this Book is of prayer. Indeed, it could be viewed as a treatise on prayer vividly illustrated from life. The very name of Samuel means 'asked of God', and it is a monument to a prayer presented and granted. Here we see prayer offered at all times. Therefore, we take the chief message of the book to be the place for, and the power of prayer in all experiences of life."
Robert Lee

"For sheer interest, 1 Samuel is unsurpassed. Not only does it record eventful history; it is eventful history interwoven with the biographies of three colorful personalities—Samuel, Saul, and David."
J. Sidlow Baxter

"'Behold, I have played the fool.' This is the whole story of man."
G. Campbell Morgan

NOTABLE NOTES

The story of the witch at En Dor, whom Saul consulted in chapter 28, has intrigued and puzzled students for years. It is the only instance in Scripture in which God allowed the actual spirit of one of His people to ascend out of the earth and to speak "from the dead."

CHRIST CONNECTIONS

Christ can be found in 1 Samuel as:

Anointed Prophet and Priest

True Claimant to the Scepter of Judah and Throne of David

2 SAMUEL

IMPORTANT INFORMATION

AUTHOR: **Nathan and Gad**

THEME: **The History of David's Kingdom**

CATEGORY: **History**

FASCINATING FACTS

1. 2 Samuel is devoted almost entirely to the history of David as king.

2. David's name appears 1,118 times in Scripture, second only to the name of Jesus. His name appears 280 times in 2 Samuel.

3. 2 Samuel gives us the first instance in which a ruler was compared to a shepherd (5:2).

4. 2 Samuel contains two notable parables, in particular, Nathan's parable that exposed David's sin (12:1–12; 14:1–20).

5. In 2 Samuel, David claims divine inspiration of his writings (23:2).

6. 2 Samuel is a powerful picture of the New Testament truth stated in James 1:15 about the effects of sin.

7. 2 Samuel records the establishment of Jerusalem as the Holy City of God.

8. While Samuel's name appears at least 130 times in 1 Samuel, it does not appear once in the book of 2 Samuel.

9. The Books of 1 and 2 Samuel were originally one single book in the old Hebrew Bible, which was simply called the book of Samuel.

10. David, the son of Jesse, is the only person in the Bible to bear that name, which means "beloved."

QUOTABLE QUOTES

"The story of the second book of Samuel is one of triumph and tragedy, the rise and decline of King David, the triumph of his public life and the tragedy of his private one."
Eric W. Hayden

"The book [of 2 Samuel] teaches us first that God's opportunity is created by the attitude of man towards Him; and secondly, that man's opportunity is created by the attitude of God towards him."
G. Campbell Morgan

"The Bible never flatters its heroes...As we consider the record of Bible characters, how often we find ourselves looking into a mirror. We are humiliated by the reminder of how many times we have failed. Great has been our stubbornness but greater still has been His faithfulness. Nowhere is this more true than in the story of the life of David."
Alan Redpath

NOTABLE NOTES

In 2 Samuel 3:1–5, six of David's sons are named, and each one was born to a different wife! Unlike most of the other future rulers of Israel, David's sins never included idolatry. However, they did include polygamy.

CHRIST CONNECTIONS

Christ can be found in 2 Samuel as:
Son of David
Greater David

1 KINGS

IMPORTANT INFORMATION

AUTHOR: **Probably Jeremiah**

THEME **Sin Brings Division**

CATEGORY: **History**

FASCINATING FACTS

1. 1 Kings opens and closes with death: it opens with the death of David (2:10) and closes with the death of Ahab (22:37).

2. 1 Kings opens with Israel as one kingdom, and closes with Israel as two kingdoms.

3. 1 Kings records the shortest reign of any earthly king, which was seven days (16:15, Zimri).

4. Solomon was wiser than anyone who has ever lived (4:31). He spoke 3,000 proverbs and wrote 1,005 songs (4:32).

5. 1 Kings contains Scripture's first record of a bodily resurrection from the dead (17:22).

6. The building of the first of three temples is recorded in 1 Kings.

7. Solomon was the foremost polygamist in the Bible, with 700 wives and 300 concubines (11:3).

8. 1 Kings records the first instance of someone kneeling in prayer (8:54, Solomon).

9. The word "king" appears some 250 times in this book.

10. 1 Kings contains the first recorded instances of someone taking hold of the horns of the altar for refuge and protection (1:50; 2:28).

11. Israel's land size was the largest ever during the reign of Solomon (4:24).

12. Two well-known female characters from 1 Kings, Jezebel and the queen of Sheba, are referenced in the New Testament to make important spiritual points (Revelation 2:20; Matthew 12:42).

QUOTABLE QUOTES

"These books [1 and 2 Kings] present God as sovereign over all man's affairs, God as faithful to His people, and man as responsible for his actions."
Richard I. McNeely

"These are the two most important books of history in the world. Every day expeditions are digging up the records of history about which nothing has been written outside the books of the Kings."
Henrietta C. Mears

"The best part of a good story is its conclusion. The reason is that a story is like a giant puzzle. Story elements—exciting action, conflicts between characters, lovely landscapes—sketch in 'pieces' of the scene. Only at the end, however, when the last 'piece' falls into place, does the whole finished picture appear. First Kings provides the preliminary pieces of Israel's life under the monarchy."
Robert L. Hubbard, Jr.

NOTABLE NOTES

The wealth of King Solomon was staggering. It included billions of dollars in gold, 40,000 horses, 1,400 chariots, an extensive fleet of ships, and an ivory throne overlaid in gold and surrounded by twelve statues of lions!

CHRIST CONNECTIONS

Christ can be found in 1 Kings as:
The Only Perfect King
Greater Solomon
Builder of God's Temple

2 KINGS

IMPORTANT INFORMATION

AUTHOR: **Probably Jeremiah**

THEME: **Sin Brings Discipline**

CATEGORY: **History**

FASCINATING FACTS

1. 2 Kings records the longest reign of any earthly king: fifty-five years (21:1, Manasseh).

2. 2 Kings references the only naturally bald man in Scripture: Elisha (2:23).

3. 2 Kings records one of only two people in the Bible who did not die: Elijah (2:11; Enoch was the other; see Genesis 5).

4. 2 Kings records the account of the only woman who ever ruled Judah, a wicked and murderous woman named Athaliah (chapter 11).

5. During the period of 2 Kings, the following prophets all prophesied: Amos, Hosea, Obadiah, Joel, Isaiah, Micah, Nahum, Habakkuk, Zephaniah, and Jeremiah.

6. 2 Kings records two of the three bodily resurrections found in the Old Testament (4:34–35; 13:20–21).

7. Half of 2 Kings deals with the life and ministry of just one man: Elisha, the prophet.

8. In 2 Kings, we read that a king "did evil in the sight of the Lord" twenty-one times, and only eight times do we read that any kings "did what was right in the sight of the Lord."

9. 2 Kings covers a time period of about 270 years, or more than twice the period of time in 1 Kings.

10. 2 Kings records the two instances in which God parted the waters of the Jordan River.

11. There is not a single instance of failure recorded in the ministry of Elisha.

12. In 2 Kings 19 and 20, the prophet Isaiah is referred to some thirteen times.

QUOTABLE QUOTES

"As Elijah's mighty works were very much the glory of the former book, towards the latter end of it, so were Elisha's the glory of this one, towards the beginning of it. These prophets out-shone their princes; and therefore, as far as they go, the history shall be accounted for in them."
Matthew Henry

"In the days when Josiah carried out his reformation, the book of the Law was found. Mark the significance of this fact that it had to be found! Moreover, its teaching so astonished Josiah that he halted in the middle of his work to inquire from the prophetess Huldah. The people had so forgotten the law of their God that, when it was found, they were absolutely unfamiliar with it."
G. Campbell Morgan

"The second book of Kings has been much more extensively confirmed and illustrated through recent research than any other book of the Old Testament. This is due to the fact that the annals of Assyria and of Babylon, covering the same period of 2 Kings, have been so largely recovered...could there be any fuller proof of reliability?"
John Urquhart

NOTABLE NOTES

When Elijah prepared to depart for heaven in 2 Kings 2, his servant and succeeding prophet, Elisha, asked that a double portion of his spirit be upon him (2:9). As it turned out, Elisha did indeed perform twice as many miracles as his mentor Elijah. The only other person in Scripture who did more miracles than Elisha was Jesus!

CHRIST CONNECTIONS

Christ can be found in 2 Kings as:
The Only Perfect King
Man of God and Word of God

1 CHRONICLES

IMPORTANT INFORMATION

AUTHOR: **Ezra**

THEME: **A Spiritual Perspective**

CATEGORY: **History**

FASCINATING FACTS

1. Chronicles contains the shortest verse in the Old Testament (1:25) and one of the strangest verses (26:18).

2. 1 and 2 Chronicles make more mention of non-biblical books (twelve) than any other books in the Bible (i.e., book of Nathan, book of Gad, etc.).

3. 1 and 2 Chronicles review the history of man from Adam to Cyrus, covering a period of about 3,500 years.

4. 1 Chronicles contains the only recorded instance of someone sitting down while praying (17:16).

5. 1 Chronicles contains far more listings of genealogies than are found in any other book of the Bible.

6. 1 Chronicles 21:1 refers to Satan by name for the first time in Scripture.

7. 1 Chronicles is not directly quoted anywhere in the New Testament.

8. The first nine chapters of 1 Chronicles are the most extensive listings of genealogies in the Bible.

9. "Seek the Lord" is a recurring statement and theme in 1 Chronicles.

10. The name "David" is recorded more than 180 times in this book.

QUOTABLE QUOTES

"The history of the chosen people is related afresh in a new manner, and from a new standpoint. While the same events are recorded, they are viewed from a different standpoint. In Samuel and Kings we have the facts of history; here we have the divine words and thoughts about these facts. In the former books they are regarded from a man's standpoint; here they are viewed from a divine standpoint."
E. W. Bullinger

"The book of Chronicles is occupied from beginning to end with magnifying God, and giving Him His right place in Israel."
Robert Lee

"First impressions can be misleading. In the case of Chronicles they usually are...What seems at a casual glance to be a re-telling of Samuel/Kings turns out to be something more than a mere repeat...Its object is the fostering of a right relationship between God and His people."
Michael Wilcox

NOTABLE NOTES

The familiar story of David numbering the tribes and bringing grave consequences upon the people as a result of his sin is recorded in chapter 21. The threshing floor of Ornan that David bought and where he offered a sacrifice was located on Mount Moriah. This was the same place where Abraham offered up his son Isaac (Genesis 22:2), and where Solomon later built the temple (2 Chronicles 3:1). The Jews believe that the altar of burnt offering in the temple at Jerusalem was situated on the exact site of the altar on which Abraham intended to sacrifice Isaac. Today, the Muslim mosque, the Dome of the Rock in Jerusalem, is situated on this site.

CHRIST CONNECTIONS

Christ can be found in 1 Chronicles as:
The Reigning King

2 CHRONICLES

IMPORTANT INFORMATION

AUTHOR: Ezra

THEME: God Keeps His Word

CATEGORY: History

FASCINATING FACTS

1. 2 Chronicles records the largest army actually ever assembled: one million (14:9).

2. 2 Chronicles records the youngest king who ever ruled, Joash, who was only seven years old (24:1)!

3. 1 and 2 Chronicles heavily emphasize the various elements of worship: the temple, its services, priests, Levites, singers, musicians, and so on.

4. 2 Chronicles opens with the building of the first temple and closes with the decree to rebuild the second temple.

5. 2 Chronicles is not directly quoted anywhere in the New Testament.

6. 2 Chronicles 33 records the conversion of Israel's most wicked king: Manasseh.

7. 2 Chronicles is the last book of the Hebrew Bible.

8. 2 Chronicles ends with Israel going into their Babylonian captivity. After their restoration from that captivity, Judah never worshiped idols again!

9. The closing verses of 2 Chronicles (36:22–23) are also the opening verses of Ezra (1:1–3).

11. In 2 Chronicles, the word "house," referring to the house of the Lord, is mentioned nearly 150 times.

QUOTABLE QUOTES

"1 and 2 Chronicles are the 'epitome of the Old Testament.'"
Jerome

"Put all this together, and the truth of the Word of God will appear, those who honor Me I will honor, but those who despise Me shall be lightly esteemed."
Matthew Henry

"The message of Chronicles is 'messianic'; that is, it looks forward to the coming King who will rule over God's people forever...In the New Testament, we learn that this King's name is Jesus."
John Sailhamer

NOTABLE NOTES

2 Chronicles 32 records the story of Hezekiah's tunnel. The king wanted to have water provisions available for the city in the case of an outside siege or attack. This 1,700 foot-long tunnel brought in water from the Gihon Spring in the Kidron Valley to Jerusalem. In 1880 a young boy discovered the old tunnel while he was playing in the water. The tunnel still functions today, and if you visit Jerusalem, you can walk inside of it.

CHRIST CONNECTIONS

Christ can be found in 2 Chronicles as:
The Perfect King, Priest, and Prophet

EZRA

AUTHOR: **Ezra**

THEME: **The Word of the Lord**

CATEGORY: **History**

FASCINATING FACTS

1. The book of Ezra records no miracles.

2. Ezra was one of the last Old Testament authors.

3. Ezra is one of two books in the Bible that carries a significant amount of original material in Aramaic (see also: Daniel).

4. The book of Ezra records the building of the second temple of God in Jerusalem.

5. The book of Ezra is never quoted anywhere in the New Testament.

6. Ezra records the first two of three returns of Jewish exiles from Babylon to Jerusalem.

7. Ezra is the only scribe to author a book of the Bible.

8. Ezra is the only book that begins with virtually the same final words of another book (compare 2 Chronicles 36:22–23 with Ezra 1:1–3).

9. Ezra has the unusual feature of having an almost sixty-year break between its two main divisions (chapters 1–6; 7–10).

10. Ezra 7:21 contains all of the letters of the alphabet except the letter "j."

11. The name of Jerusalem appears some forty-seven times in this book.

12. Jewish tradition and the Talmud claim that Ezra was responsible for helping to put the Old Testament canon together.

QUOTABLE QUOTES

"That the book of Ezra contains much-needed truth for the present time is my firm belief."
Harry A. Ironside

"The book of Ezra is a work of so simple a character as scarcely to require an 'introduction.' It is a plain and straightforward account of one of the most important events in Jewish history—the return of the people of God from the Babylonian captivity...No book of Scripture has fewer difficulties or obscurities. There is no miracle recorded in it, hence its historical truth is admitted almost universally."
The Pulpit Commentary

"Ezra is often called 'the Father of Judaism'...The rabbinic tradition praised Ezra highly; he is mentioned often in the Talmud. He was considered a man of the Torah, as was Moses. It was observed that if Moses had not preceded him, Ezra would have received the Torah straight from Yahweh. Further, whereas God had given the Torah to the people through Moses, at a later time, when the Torah was largely forgotten, Ezra acted to reestablish it in the Jewish community."
Fredrick Carlson Holmgren

NOTABLE NOTES

Ezra has been called, next to Moses, "The Second Lawgiver," because he brought the Law of Moses back to the people. In addition, the book of Ezra has been called "The Second Great Exodus." Just as, in the book of Exodus, Israel left slavery in Egypt to go and worship the Lord in their new homeland; so too, in the book of Ezra, Israel left captivity in Babylon to go and worship the Lord in their homeland!

CHRIST CONNECTIONS

Christ can be found in Ezra as:
Faithful Scribe
Builder and Restorer of the Church

NEHEMIAH

AUTHOR: Ezra and/or Nehemiah

THEME: Prayer and Perseverance

CATEGORY: History

FASCINATING FACTS

1. Nehemiah contains the longest prayer in the Old Testament (9:5–38).

2. Nehemiah begins and ends with prayer, and throughout the book, is filled with twelve instances of prayers.

3. Chronologically, Nehemiah is the last historical book of the Old Testament.

4. Nehemiah was the most autobiographical of the historical writers.

5. Nehemiah's life is one of the very best examples of spiritual leadership in the Bible.

6.   The decree of King Artaxerxes in Nehemiah 2:8 is the beginning of Daniel's famous Seventy Weeks (Daniel 9:25–27).

7.   The person of Nehemiah is not mentioned anywhere else in Scripture outside of this book.

8.   Nehemiah is never quoted anywhere in the New Testament.

9.   The prophet Malachi was a contemporary of Nehemiah's and helped to rebuke the sins of the people in Jerusalem.

10. Nehemiah prayed and fasted for four months and then led in the difficult task of rebuilding the wall around Jerusalem in only fifty-two days! (6:15).

11. The word "build" is used nearly two dozen times in this book.

QUOTABLE QUOTES

"Let us learn this lesson from Nehemiah: you never lighten the load unless you first have felt the pressure in your own soul. You are never used of God to bring blessing until God has opened your eyes and made you see things as they really are. There is no other preparation for Christian work than that. Nehemiah was called to build the wall, but first he had to weep over the ruins."
Alan Redpath

"[Nehemiah's] achievements were as outstanding as his gifts. He rebuilt the ruined wall of Jerusalem in fifty-two days, when nobody else thought it could be rebuilt at all...He takes his place, by right, as it seems to me, with the greatest leaders of God's people in the Bible story—with Moses and

David and Paul. Nehemiah was truly a marvelous man."
J. I. Packer

"May God, who raised up Nehemiah, raise up many like him in our day. The church has seldom been in greater need of such leaders."
James Montgomery Boice

"Nehemiah, although an ordinary man underneath, emerges as one of the most significant leaders in history. He was highly motivated to do a job for God that had many difficult circumstances surrounding it." **Charles R. Swindoll**

NOTABLE NOTES

In the book of Joshua, Joshua was called by the Lord to bring down a wall around Jericho. In the book of Nehemiah, Nehemiah was called by the Lord to raise up a wall around Jerusalem. Both were godly men and godly leaders, but were called to opposite tasks!

CHRIST CONNECTIONS

Christ can be found in Nehemiah as:
Rebuilder of the Broken Walls
Governor of the Church
Restorer and Protector

ESTHER

IMPORTANT INFORMATION

AUTHOR: **Unknown**

THEME: **The Providence of God**

CATEGORY: **History**

FASCINATING FACTS

1. Esther is the third of four Old Testament books whose author is unknown (see also: Judges, Ruth, and Job).

2. Esther is the second of only two books in the Bible named after a woman (see also: Ruth).

3. Esther is the first of only two books in the Bible that does not mention God by name or the title of "Lord" (see also: Song of Solomon).

4. Esther is the one book in the Bible devoted entirely to the providence of God.

5.   Esther is the only book that gives us the origin of the Feast of Purim (chapter 9), or that even mentions this festival.

6.   Esther contains the longest single verse in the Bible: Esther 8:9 (ninety words).

7.   The book of Esther is never quoted or alluded to in the New Testament

8.   Esther's story takes place in Persia and gives us a window into the customs and culture of the Persian Empire.

9.   The book of Esther contains no recorded miracles and yet the entire story, knit together, is a very miraculous story.

10.   The book of Esther is a clear illustration of God's promise made to Abraham and his descendants in Genesis 12:3: "I will bless those who bless you, and I will curse him who curses you."

11.   Reference to "the Jews" is made forty-three times in this book

QUOTABLE QUOTES

"An alternative title for the book of Esther might well be 'The Romance of Providence,' for providence might be said to be the key word by which to remember the main theme and teaching. God is certainly out of sight, hidden, unrecognized, but He is all the time at work, completing His plan and purpose for individuals, nations, and the universe."
A. T. Pierson

"Esther could be compared to a chess game. God and Satan (as invisible players) moved real kings, queens, and nobles. When Satan put Hamaan into place, it was

as if he announced 'Check.' God then positioned Esther and Mordecai in order to put Satan into 'Checkmate'!"
John MacArthur Jr.

"If the name of God is not here, His finger is."
Matthew Henry

"Tucked away in the Bible in an obscure corner of the Old Testament is the little book of Esther...It is a gripping tale, but one might rather expect to find it in the pages of Reader's Digest than the Bible."
Ray C. Stedman

NOTABLE NOTES

When the book of Esther is read every year at the Feast of Purim, and the name of Hamaan is read, the people respond by stomping their feet on the floor and saying, "Let his name be blotted out! The name of the wicked will rot!" Oftentimes, the children will have special Purim rattles and will shake them every time they hear Hamaan's name read. Then, at the end of the reading, the people say, "Cursed be Hamaan; blessed be Mordecai!"

CHRIST CONNECTIONS

Christ can be found in Esther as:
Our Mordecai
Our Advocate

JOB

IMPORTANT INFORMATION

AUTHOR: Unknown

THEME: Man's Suffering–God's Sovereignty

CATEGORY: Wisdom

FASCINATING FACTS

1. Job is considered by many to be the oldest book of the Bible and, very possibly, the oldest book in the world.

2. Job is the fourth of four Old Testament books in which its author is unknown (see also: Judges, Ruth, and Esther).

3. The book of Job refers to Satan by name more times than any other book in the Bible (14 times).

4. The book of Job uses the name of "Almighty" (Shaddai) for God more times than any other book in the Bible (31 times).

5. Job is the only book in the Bible that makes references to what

many believe were the dinosaurs (behemoth, 40:15; leviathan, 41:1).

6. Job contains the only recorded conversation in heaven between God and Satan in Scripture (chapter 1).

7. Job is the one book in the Bible largely devoted to the subject of human suffering.

8. Job contains far more archaic language than any other book in the Bible, because it is an ancient book.

9. Sixteen times in this book, Job asks God the question, "Why?"

10. In Job 38–41, God confronts Job with at least seventy-five questions of His own!

11. The book of Job is directly quoted twice in the New Testament (Romans 11:35, 1 Corinthians 3:19), and both Ezekiel (14:14) and James (5:11) refer to the person of Job.

12. The final five chapters of Job give us a significant overview of God's Creation.

QUOTABLE QUOTES

"Though the book is ancient, its insights are remarkably modern, and its message is needed more today than ever before."
Henry M. Morris

"[Job is] more magnificent and sublime than any other book of Scripture."
Martin Luther

"I call this book, apart from all theories about it, one of the grandest things ever written with pen...There is nothing written, I think, in the Bible or out of it, of equal literary merit."
Thomas Carlyle

"The book of Job is perhaps the greatest masterpiece of the human mind."
Victor Hugo

NOTABLE NOTES

The book of Job contains an intriguing recurrence of the numbers seven and three: seven sons and three daughters; 7,000 sheep and 3,000 camels; three friends who sat with Job for seven days, and so on.

CHRIST CONNECTIONS

Christ can be found in Job as:
Ever-Living Redeemer

PSALMS

IMPORTANT INFORMATION

AUTHOR: **David and Others**

THEME: **Praise and Worship**

CATEGORY: **Wisdom**

FASCINATING FACTS

1. Psalms is the longest book in the Bible.

2. Psalms contains the longest (119) and the shortest (117) chapters in the Bible.

3. Psalms is the most quoted Old Testament book in the New Testament, and Psalm 110:1 is the most quoted Old Testament verse in the New Testament.

4. Psalm 117 is the middle chapter of the Bible (out of 1,189 total).

5. Psalms is the most Messianic of the Old Testament books.

6. Jesus quoted from Psalms at the beginning and at the end of His ministry (John 2:17; Luke 23:46).

7. Almost every psalm contains some note of praise to God.

8. Psalm 23 is one of the most familiar, best-known, and well-loved passages of Scripture.

9. No other book of the Bible is so filled with devotional material and expressions as Psalms.

10. Every great doctrine in the Bible is taught, expressed, or implied in Psalms.

11. One hundred of the 150 psalms identify the author's name.

12. Of the 150 psalms in this book, about half identify David as the writer.

13. Every attribute or characteristic of God's divine nature is found in the Psalms.

14. The word "praise" is used over 175 times throughout Psalms.

15. The book of Psalms is the best example in the Bible of the nature of Hebrew poetry.

16. In Psalms, the word "salvation" is found over sixty times, more than twice that of any other book in the Bible.

17. Psalms is the only book in the Bible that begins with the word "blessed."

18. Psalms has more authors than any other book in the Bible.

19. Psalms is the only book of the Bible quoted by Satan (in Matthew 4:6 Satan quotes Psalm 91:11–12).

"In this book of Psalms the tempted and the tested gain fortitude from pilgrims of yesterday, whose feet have bled along the same thorny pathway."
J. Sidlow Baxter

"Although all Scripture breathes the grace of God, yet sweet beyond all others is the book of Psalms. History instructs, the Law teaches, Prophecy announces, rebukes, chastens, Morality persuades; but in the book of Psalms we have the fruit of all these, and a kind of medicine for the salvation of men."
Ambrose of Milan

"Moses gave to the Israelites the five books of the Law; and David gave them the five books of the Psalms."
Ancient Jewish Statement

"He that would be wise, let him read the Proverbs; He that would be holy, let him read the Psalms."
R. Steele

NOTABLE NOTES

C. H. Spurgeon's greatest written work was undoubtedly *The Treasury of David*, his extensive commentary on the book of Psalms, which took him over twenty years to research and write. It sold over 148,000 copies while Spurgeon was still alive! After completing it, Spurgeon said, "A tinge of sadness is on my spirit as I quit *The Treasury of David*, never to find on this earth a richer storehouse...Blessed have been the days spent in meditating, mourning, hoping, believing, and exulting with David."

CHRIST CONNECTIONS

Christ can be found in Psalms as:
Our Shepherd
All in All

PROVERBS

IMPORTANT INFORMATION

AUTHOR: **Solomon**

THEME: **The Wisdom of God**

CATEGORY: **Wisdom**

FASCINATING FACTS

1. Proverbs is one of three books written by Solomon, whom the Bible calls the wisest man to ever live (1 Kings 3:12).

2. The author of Proverbs, Solomon, wrote 3,000 proverbs and compiled 1,005 songs (1 Kings 4:32).

3. Proverbs contains the longest introduction of any Old Testament book.

4. In Proverbs, the words "wise" and "wisdom" are used at least 125 times.

5. There are at least eighteen references in Proverbs to "the fear of the Lord," which is the beginning of wisdom (1:7).

6. In the New Testament, Proverbs is quoted more than twenty times.

7.   Less than 800 of Solomon's 3,000 proverbs are found in this book.

8.   Proverbs is one of just a few books in Scripture that clearly describes its purpose (1:2–6).

9.   The title of "Lord" (Jehovah) is never used in any of Solomon's three books, though "God" is used over eight times in this book.

10. Proverbs is perhaps the most practical book in the Bible for everyday living, touching on nearly 100 topics.

11. Proverbs, more than any other book in the Bible, addresses youth with instruction and direction.

12. Proverbs contains the most graphic and comprehensive description of the ill effects of alcohol found anywhere in Scripture (23:29–35).

QUOTABLE QUOTES

"The book of Proverbs is about godly wisdom, how to get it, and how to use it. It's about priorities and principles, not get-rich-quick schemes or success formulas. It tells you, not how to make a living, but how to be skillful in the lost art of making a life."
Warren W. Wiersbe

"A proverb is a wise saying in which a few words are chosen instead of many, with a design to condense wisdom into a brief form both to aid memory and stimulate study...Only profound meditation will reveal what is hidden in these moral and spiritual maxims."
A. T. Pierson

"The book of Proverbs is the kind of biblical fare you should indulge in often, but not in large doses. The 'stuff' of Proverbs has already been distilled so that its advice comes to us in highly concentrated form. These sage tidbits have been boiled down, trimmed, honed, polished, and sharpened to where a little goes a long way."
Robert L. Alden

NOTABLE NOTES

It has been pointed out in Jewish thinking that Solomon wrote three books at three different points in his life. He wrote Song of Solomon as a young man in love. Then he wrote the book of Proverbs as a middle-aged man in wisdom. Finally, he wrote Ecclesiastes as an older man in his later years after learning many of life's lessons the hard way.

CHRIST CONNECTIONS

Christ can be found in Proverbs as:
Wisdom of God

ECCLESIASTES

IMPORTANT INFORMATION

AUTHOR: **Solomon**

THEME: **The Meaning of Life**

CATEGORY: **Wisdom**

FASCINATING FACTS

1.   Ecclesiastes is one of three books written by Solomon, the wisest and wealthiest man who ever lived (see also: Proverbs and Song of Solomon).

2.   Ecclesiastes is the most philosophical of all the books in the Bible.

3.   Ecclesiastes is the only book aimed directly at the question of the meaning of life.

4.   In Ecclesiastes, the word "vanity" is found thirty-seven times.

5.   In Ecclesiastes, the phrase "under the sun" appears twenty-nine times.

6. Ecclesiastes contains virtually no history and no significant stories or parables.

7. Ecclesiastes is more pessimistic in perspective than any other Book in the Bible.

8. Ecclesiastes contains the most picturesque description of old age in Scripture (12:1–7).

9. Ecclesiastes contains a remarkable number of scientifically accurate statements.

10. The word "wisdom" is used twenty-eight times in this book.

QUOTABLE QUOTES

"It is the message that everything on earth, even at its best, is fleeting and unsatisfying, and that the heart of man was made for God and will not find rest and satisfaction till it finds realization in Him who is changeless, absolute, and permanent."
Merrill F. Unger

"You do not have to go outside the Bible to find the merely human philosophy of life. God has given us the book of Ecclesiastes, the record of all that human thinking and natural religion has ever been able to discover concerning the meaning and goal of life."
Henrietta Mears

"Whether prose or verse, I know nothing grander in its impassioned survey of mortal pain and pleasure, its estimate of failure and success; none of more notable sadness; no poem working more indomitably for spiritual illumination."
Ray C. Stedman

NOTABLE NOTES

Ecclesiastes is a part of the Old Testament books of the Megilloth, or "scrolls," which includes Ruth, Esther, Song of Solomon, and Lamentations. These books were read both publicly and privately at the various Jewish feasts. Publicly, the Rabbis would read from these five books in the synagogue on five special occasions during the year: Ruth was read at Pentecost; Esther at Purim; Ecclesiastes at Tabernacles; Song of Solomon at Passover; and Lamentations was read in remembrance of Nebuchadnezzar's destruction of Jerusalem.

CHRIST CONNECTIONS

Christ can be found in Ecclesiastes as:
Wisdom of God
Preacher
Son of David
King of Jerusalem

SONG OF SOLOMON

IMPORTANT INFORMATION

AUTHOR: **Solomon**

THEME: **Marital Love**

CATEGORY: **Wisdom**

FASCINATING FACTS

1. The Song of Solomon is the only book of the Bible that is completely devoted to the subject of marital love.

2. Song of Solomon is the second of only two books in the Bible that does not mention God by name or use the title of "Lord" (see also: Esther).

3. The Song of Solomon is never quoted or alluded to in the New Testament, nor is it quoted in the other books of the Old Testament.

4. Song of Solomon is one of three books written by Solomon, the wisest and wealthiest man who ever lived (see also: Proverbs and Ecclesiastes).

5.　The Song of Solomon refers to twenty-one different varieties of plants, fifteen species of animals, and fifteen geographic locations.

6.　The Song of Solomon is one of two books in Scripture that has routinely been labeled by nonbelievers as fictional and not factual (see also: Jonah).

7.　The Song of Solomon was one of the most challenged books for inclusion into the Old Testament canon of Scripture.

8.　The Song of Solomon records nearly fifty words that are not found anywhere else in Scripture.

9.　The Song of Solomon has thirty-two occurrences of the word "beloved."

10.　The Song of Solomon was sometimes referred to as the "Canticles," which is the Latin word for "songs."

 ## QUOTABLE QUOTES

"The Song occupies a sacred enclosure into which none may enter unprepared...the holy of holies, before which the veil still hangs to many an untaught believer."
C. H. Spurgeon

"Solomon calls this book 'the Song of Songs.' In the temple there was a holy of holies; Jesus stands among men as the King of kings; in the universe there is a heaven of heavens. And among the poetical books of the Word of God there is a song of songs."
John Phillips

"It is well that Ecclesiastes is followed by the Song of Solomon, for the one is the complement of the other. In Ecclesiastes we learn that without Christ we cannot be satisfied, even if we possess the whole world—the heart is too large for the object. In the Song of Solomon we learn that if we turn from the world and set our affections on Christ, we cannot fathom the infinite preciousness of His love—the Object is too large for the heart."
Robert Lee

NOTABLE NOTES

The Song of Solomon has been the favorite book of the Bible with some of the most famous men of God. That list includes C. H. Spurgeon, D. L. Moody, and Hudson Taylor.

CHRIST CONNECTIONS

Christ can be found in Song of Solomon as:
Perfect Lover and Bridegroom
King of Peace

ISAIAH

AUTHOR: Isaiah

THEME: The Salvation of God

CATEGORY: Major Prophet

FASCINATING FACTS

1. The book of Isaiah is a picture of the entire Bible in miniature form, containing sixty-six chapters (compare with 66 books of the Bible) and with two main sections of thirty-nine chapters and twenty-seven chapters (compare with 39 books of the Old Testament and 27 books of the New Testament).

2. The reference to God as the "Holy One of Israel" is used over thirty times in the book of Isaiah.

3. Isaiah contains the longest name or word found in Scripture, the name belonging to the son of Isaiah: "Mahershalalhashbaz" (8:1).

4. Isaiah is the most-quoted Old Testament prophet in the New Testament.

5. The prophet Isaiah is mentioned by name twenty-one times in the New Testament.

6. Isaiah contains the only Old Testament prophecy of the virgin birth of Christ (7:14).

7. Isaiah contains more references to the coming Savior than any other book of the Bible.

8. Isaiah was married to a woman who also prophesied (8:3).

9. Isaiah was the most evangelical of all the prophets.

10. The name "Isaiah" means "Salvation of God," and the word "salvation" is found nearly thirty times, second only to the book of Psalms.

11. Isaiah is the longest prophetic book of the Old Testament.

12. Isaiah presents more insights into the nature of God than any other book of the Old Testament.

13. When Jesus began His public ministry, He quoted from chapter sixty-one of Isaiah in fulfillment of that prophecy (Luke 4:18).

14. In Isaiah, the phrase "For the mouth of the Lord has spoken it" is found three times (and nowhere else) in Scripture.

15. Isaiah prophesied during the reigns of five kings of Judah: Uzziah, Jotham, Ahaz, Hezekiah, and Manasseh.

16. Isaiah is one of two Old Testament books (see also: Ezekiel) that records the origin of Satan's fall (14:12–14).

17. Isaiah 53, the key chapter in this book, is quoted or alluded to more than eighty-five times in the New Testament.

18. Isaiah contains the only reference in Scripture in which the "seraphim" angels are mentioned specifically by name (6:2, 6).

19. There are seven things that are called "everlasting" in Isaiah: salvation, light, joy, strength, kindness, covenant, and judgment.

20. Only in Isaiah is Satan called "Lucifer," which means "bright one" or "bearer of light" (14:12).

21. Zion is mentioned more times in Isaiah than in any other book of the Bible.

QUOTABLE QUOTES

"Isaiah was a princely character, a wise and patriotic statesman, a gifted poet, and a divinely inspired prophet. He may not have been of noble birth, as some have supposed; but his heroic courage, his spotless purity, his sympathy with the poor, his hatred of sham and pretense, his exalted ideas and his unfailing faith in God gave him a more royal rank than any kingly pedigree could have conferred."
Charles R. Erdman

"Never perhaps has there been another prophet like Isaiah, who stood with his head in the clouds and his feet on the solid earth, with his heart in the things of eternity and his mouth and hands in the things of time, with his spirit in the eternal counsel of God and his body in the very definite moment of history. Truly, Isaiah may be called the dean of prophets."
Jan Valeton the Younger

"Hardly anyone would question the claim that Isaiah is a prince among prophets. His eloquence is very evident. His major theme is Yahweh's sovereignty. He has at his command a vocabulary richer than that of any prophet, even more comprehensive than that of the book of Psalms."
H. C. Leupold

NOTABLE NOTES

Tradition says that Isaiah was martyred by being placed inside of a hollow log and sawn in two. The wicked King Manasseh ordered this because Isaiah spoke against some of the king's acts of idolatry. If this is true, then the author of the book of Hebrews may have had Isaiah in mind in Hebrews 11:37 when he referred to the martyrs of the Christian faith who were "sawn in two."

CHRIST CONNECTIONS

Christ can be found in Isaiah as:
Messiah
Holy One of Israel
Prince of Peace
Salvation, Righteousness, and Comfort
Judge

JEREMIAH

AUTHOR: **Jeremiah**

THEME: **The Judgment of Judah**

CATEGORY: **Major Prophet**

FASCINATING FACTS

1. Jeremiah is the only major or minor prophet to author more than one book (see also: Lamentations).

2. Jeremiah was the only prophet ever instructed by God not to pray for his own nation (chapter 7).

3. The book of Jeremiah is quoted at least seven different times in the Old and New Testaments.

4. Jeremiah's calling included remaining unmarried (16:2), and he was the only man in the Bible who was told not to marry.

5. Jeremiah makes reference to Babylon (God's instrument of judgment) over 160 times, more than the rest of Scripture combined.

6.   Jeremiah was the most despised and persecuted Old Testament prophet.

7.   Jeremiah was the only prophet to give us an eyewitness account of Jerusalem's destruction (chapter 39).

8.   Jeremiah records more about his own personal life in this book than any other prophet.

9.   Jeremiah's life spanned the reigns of at least five kings in Judah: Josiah, Jehoahaz, Jehoiakim, Jehoiachin, and Zedekiah.

10.   Jeremiah 52 is almost identical to 2 Kings 24:18–25:30.

11.   Jeremiah, like the apostle Paul, was set apart before birth to serve God in a special way (Jeremiah 1:5; Galatians 1:15).

12.   The name of God as "Lord of Hosts" is found some eighty times in this book.

13.   "Backsliding" is a key word in Jeremiah, used some thirteen times.

QUOTABLE QUOTES

"Jeremiah is the most misunderstood of all the great men of history. To be one of the healthiest of men and to be thought morbid, to be one of the strongest and to be thought weak, to be one of the bravest and to be thought faint-hearted, to be a titan and to be thought a pigmy, has been his hard fortune."
Ballantine

"The book of Jeremiah is one of outstanding fascination for the Bible student for it clearly reveals the life and character of the writer, the prophet himself...Perhaps in the life of suffering we see in Jeremiah a man most near to the Man of Sorrows, the Lord Jesus Christ Himself."
Eric W. Hayden

"Jeremiah was the prophet of Judah's midnight hour."
J. Sidlow Baxter

NOTABLE NOTES

No other Old Testament prophet of God probably suffered as much as Jeremiah did during his 40 years of ministry. He often found himself standing alone and opposed by people, prophets (false), princes, and priests. He was mocked, whipped, accused, threatened, despised, hated, rejected, imprisoned, and cast into a pit. He never appears to have been free from trials and troubles during his ministry. No wonder he is well-remembered as the Weeping Prophet, and as such, was a type of Christ.

CHRIST CONNECTIONS

Christ can be found in Jeremiah as:
Righteous Branch
The Lord Our Righteousness

LAMENTATIONS

IMPORTANT INFORMATION

AUTHOR: **Jeremiah**

THEME: **Lament Over Jerusalem's Destruction**

CATEGORY: **Major Prophet**

FASCINATING FACTS

1. Lamentations is the only book in the Bible filled primarily with laments.

2. Jeremiah was the only prophet to give us an eyewitness account of Jerusalem's destruction.

3. Jeremiah is the only major or minor prophet to author more than one book (see also: Jeremiah).

4. Jeremiah, who wrote this great lament over Jerusalem, is oftentimes referred to as the "Weeping Prophet."

5. Lamentations is perhaps the most heartbreaking of all the books in the Bible, as it records "the funeral of the Holy City."

6.   Lamentations contains five complete poems, one for each chapter, with four of them being acrostics.

7.   Lamentations is the only book of the Major and Minor Prophets with an authorship not clearly identified.

8.   Every year in Israel, Lamentations is read publicly to recall the destruction of Jerusalem by Nebuchadnezzar and the Babylonians.

9.   The actual destruction of Jerusalem, which is lamented in this book, is detailed in four Old Testament passages: 2 Kings 25; 2 Chronicles 36; Jeremiah 39, 52).

10. Lamentations, more than any other book of the Bible, reveals the suffering heart of God over sin.

QUOTABLE QUOTES

"There is nothing like the Lamentations of Jeremiah in the whole world. There has been plenty of sorrow in every age, and in every land, but such another preacher and author, with such a heart for sorrow, has never again been born."
Alexander Whyte

"The touching significance of this book lies in the fact that it is the disclosure of the love and sorrow of Jehovah for the very people whom He is chastening—a sorrow wrought by the Spirit in the heart of Jeremiah."
C. I. Scofield

"It is a cloudburst of grief, a river of tears, and a sea of sobs."
J. Sidlow Baxter

"It is the wailing wall of the Bible."
J. Vernon McGee

NOTABLE NOTES

Below the hill now known as Golgotha and Calvary, just outside of Jerusalem, there is a dark incline known as "Jeremiah's Grotto." This is believed to be the location where the rejected prophet sat and observed the ruins of Jerusalem while writing the book of Lamentations. If this is true, then it is significant that Jeremiah's Grotto is located so close to the spot where the rejected Savior died for the sins of His people some six hundred years later.

CHRIST CONNECTIONS

Christ can be found in Lamentations as:
Man of Sorrows
Weeping Prophet

EZEKIEL

AUTHOR: **Ezekiel**

THEME: **The Glory of the Lord**

CATEGORY: **Major Prophet**

FASCINATING FACTS

1. Ezekiel is one of only two people in the Bible who was commanded by God to eat a scroll (John was the other; see Revelation 10:9–10).

2. Ezekiel, more than any other prophet, was called upon by God to act out his divine messages (3:26; 4:9; etc.).

3. The book of Ezekiel contains more dates than any other Old Testament prophetic book, and is therefore well-documented.

4. The book of Ezekiel contains well over sixty occurrences and/ or variations of the phrase "then they will know that I am the Lord."

5. In Ezekiel, the prophet is called "son of man" over ninety times by God, a title that Jesus used for Himself about eighty times in the Gospels.

6. Nothing else is recorded in Scripture about Ezekiel outside of his book.

7. Ezekiel and Daniel were both captives in Babylon together, and Daniel is referred to three times in this book (14:14; 14:20; 28:3).

8. Ezekiel, more than any other prophet, received his messages in visions.

9. Ezekiel is one of two Old Testament books (see also: Isaiah) containing passages that describe the fall of Satan (chapter 28), to which Jesus apparently made reference in Luke 10:18.

10. Ezekiel places great emphasis upon the personal responsibility of sin (18:4, 20–32).

11. In Ezekiel, there are at least twenty-five references to the Holy Spirit.

12. Ezekiel speaks more about Israel's days back in Egypt than any other prophet, and is the only one to speak of Israel's idolatry in Egypt and how close they were to being judged there (20:8).

13. In Ezekiel, a key phrase is "the glory of the Lord," which is used fourteen times in the first eleven chapters.

14. Ezekiel's ministry opens with a heavenly vision of God and closes with an earthly vision of God.

15. It is stated seven times in the book of Ezekiel that "the hand of the Lord" was upon the prophet.

QUOTABLE QUOTES

"Ezekiel was a Captive and in the land of a stranger. God opened heaven and gave him visions and revelations of His word and will. The hour of greatest need is the hour of Divine Presence, and Divine Strength. In the most hopeless hour of life, in the darkest and dreariest of days, in the loneliest moments of human miseries, God will be at hand to strengthen and to save."
W. G. Heslop

"Of all the prophetic books, Ezekiel is the one that has been neglected most. Many persons are repelled by the marvelous vision of the opening chapter and, finding it too difficult to understand, proceed no further; and so they lose the blessing that they would otherwise gain."
H. A. Ironside

"The visions of glory Ezekiel had belong to some of the greatest recorded in the Word of God."
Arno C. Gaebelein

NOTABLE NOTES

Because Ezekiel was a younger contemporary of the prophet Jeremiah by at least twenty years, he seems to have patterned his ministry style after Jeremiah's, or he may have even been his disciple. There are several points of Ezekiel's teachings that find their origin in Jeremiah's writings. Ironically though, there is no mention of Jeremiah anywhere in the writing of Ezekiel.

CHRIST CONNECTIONS

Christ can be found in Ezekiel as:

Four-Faced Man

Son of Man Sent to Rebellious Israel

DANIEL

IMPORTANT INFORMATION

AUTHOR: Daniel

THEME: The Sovereignty of God

CATEGORY: Major Prophet

FASCINATING FACTS

1. Daniel is the only Old Testament book that references Gabriel and Michael, the only two holy angels whose names are known to us (Daniel 8:16; 10:13).

2. Daniel is one of two books in the Bible that carries a significant amount of material in Aramaic, one of the three languages used for writing the Bible (see also: Ezra).

3. Daniel never claimed to be a prophet and is nowhere spoken of as such in the Old Testament, yet Jesus called him a "prophet" (Matthew 24:15).

4. Daniel uses the phrase "Most High" some fourteen times in this book.

5. Daniel records more about the coming Antichrist and the Tribulation Period than any other Old Testament book.

6. No failure on the part of Daniel is ever recorded in Scripture.

7. The information contained in nine of Daniel's twelve chapters revolves around various dreams and visions.

8. In Daniel 11, there are more fulfilled prophecies recorded than in any other chapter of the Bible.

9. The book of Daniel contains more fulfilled prophecies than any other book in the Bible.

10. Daniel contains the only occurrences of the word "Messiah" in the Old Testament (9:25, 26).

11. Daniel 12:1–4 is one of the most distinct passages of the Old Testament regarding the Resurrection.

12. There are a number of miraculous events recorded in Daniel, including visions, interpretation of dreams, and deliverances from death.

13. Daniel spoke and wrote while in exile, as did Ezekiel and John (Revelation).

14. Daniel's name appears some seventy-five times in this book.

QUOTABLE QUOTES

"The book of Daniel with its great prophecies, fulfilled and unfulfilled, is one of the most important portions of God's Holy Word. No other book has been so much attacked as this prophetic book. For almost 2,000 years, wicked men, heathen philosophers, and infidels have hammered away against it; but the book of Daniel has proven to be an anvil upon

which the critic's hammers have been broken into pieces."
Arno C. Gaebelein

"Outstanding among the books of the Old Testament is the book of Daniel...a mighty tonic to faith in the absolute sovereignty of God throughout the entire earth."
Lehman Strauss

"Daniel's book has a theme of such simplicity that the most brilliant minds in the world have been unable to grasp it. It is just this: God is in charge. No one understood that better than Daniel. Centuries ago he deciphered some strange signs written by an unseen hand. Today, more than any time in history, we should be able to look at our perplexing planet and say that we, too, are able to see the handwriting on the wall."
David Jeremiah

NOTABLE NOTES

There are three great "9th chapters of prayer" in the Old Testament. They include: Ezra 9, Nehemiah 9, and Daniel 9. In all three chapters, these men of purity and integrity included themselves in the sins of the people they were praying for, in spite of the fact that no failure is ever recorded about any of them!

Christ can be found in Daniel as:

Fourth Man in the Fiery Furnace

Smitten Stone That Fills the Earth

King of Kings

HOSEA

IMPORTANT INFORMATION

AUTHOR: **Hosea**

THEME: **Israel's Unfaithfulness, God's Faithful Love**

CATEGORY: **Minor Prophet**

FASCINATING FACTS

1. Hosea is one of only two major or minor prophets from the Northern Kingdom of Israel whose writings are found in Scripture (see also: Jonah).

2. Hosea is mentioned nowhere else in the Old Testament except in the first two verses of his book, but he is referenced by Paul in the New Testament (Romans 9:25).

3. More than any other Old Testament prophet, Hosea's personal circumstances mirrored his prophetic message.

4. In Hosea, the prophet makes some 150 statements concerning the sins of Israel.

5. The book of Hosea is quoted or referred to many times in the New Testament.

6. In Hosea, references to harlotry are made some fourteen times, emphasizing Israel's unfaithfulness to the Lord.

7. Hosea contains many metaphors, imageries, and allegories.

8. Based upon the information of 1:1, Hosea probably ministered longer than any other prophet, living well into his nineties.

9. Hosea was one of the last prophets to bring the Word of the Lord to the Northern Kingdom before its overthrow.

10. The book of Hosea, along with Deuteronomy and the Gospel of John, ranks as one of the greatest books in the Bible on the love of God.

QUOTABLE QUOTES

"No other messenger gives so complete an outline of the ways of God with His earthly people as does Hosea, even Daniel not excepted."
H. A. Ironside

"The language of the book is plain and frank. There is no way to tone it down. To do so is to lose the force of its message. Bear in mind that it is God's Word. Desperate circumstances call for strong measures."
K. Owen White

"Perhaps no book of the Bible reveals more clearly than this of Hosea, the travail of God over His wayward people... No prophet sounded more profound depths of anguish in proclaiming the warning of impending judgment than Hosea; none pleaded with an apostate people more poignantly."
Herbert F. Stevenson

NOTABLE NOTES

Hosea's marriage to a prostitute named Gomer has been one of the most debated events recorded in Scripture. Some believe that the circumstances were merely allegorical and did not actually take place. Others believe that the two were married, and that Gomer became a prostitute only after her marriage to Hosea. Still others believe that Hosea married Gomer not realizing that she already was a prostitute. Finally, there are those who argue that Hosea knowingly married Gomer the harlot in obedience to God's direct command, to illustrate the unfaithfulness of Israel as a nation and its sin against God.

CHRIST CONNECTIONS

Christ can be found in Hosea as:
Patient Bridegroom
Healer of the Backslider

JOEL

AUTHOR: Joel

THEME: The Day of the Lord

CATEGORY: Minor Prophet

FASCINATING FACTS

1. It is believed that Joel was the first prophet, major or minor, to write his words.

2. Joel is one of two books in the Minor Prophets that deals almost exclusively with the coming Day of the Lord (see also: Zephaniah).

3. Joel is quoted by Peter during the Apostle's famous sermon on the Day of Pentecost (Acts 2:16–21).

4. In the book of Joel, disaster is a recurring theme: locusts, famine, fire, and so on.

5.   In Joel, while the warning of judgment for sin is clear, there is no mention of any specific sins.

6.   Joel gives us the grandest description in all of literature of a locust invasion.

7.   Joel gives us the first reference in Scripture to the outpouring of the Holy Spirit upon all flesh (2:28–29).

8.   In Joel, the range of prophecies extend from the prophet's own day until the end of time.

9.   In Joel, the phrase "Day of the Lord" is used five times, more often than in any other book of the Bible.

10. Joel makes many references to nature and agriculture.

QUOTABLE QUOTES

"It seems strange that so few of God's people read and prayerfully study these great prophetic visions. Of all generations we are the most privileged living in these significant days, standing on the threshold of the fulfillment of these predictions. We behold in our day how everything is shaping for the great events with which this present age will close. The study of the sublime, God-breathed utterances of Joel is indeed of great value and help to those who truly wait for His Son from heaven."
Arno C. Gaebelein

"As we meditate on this marvelous disclosure in God's Word, we are driven to the question, How far off can it be? Not very far!"
Charles L. Feinberg

"Joel, like most of the Old Testament prophets, consists largely of vivid poetry...Joel moves his readers from horror and hopelessness to mourning and repentance, dread and awe, joy and assurance, hope and expectation ...Obviously one needs to approach the book with imagination and sensitivity for its poetic features."
Thomas J. Finley

NOTABLE NOTES

The book of Joel presents a literal and devastating swarm of locusts with prophetic implications. In doing so, Joel bridges the book of Exodus, with its literal swarm of locusts that came in the form of the eighth plague from God and against the Egyptians (Exodus 10), and the book of Revelation, with its prophetic description of demonic "locust-like" creatures that will torment mankind for five months during the Tribulation Period (Revelation 9).

CHRIST CONNECTIONS

Christ can be found in Joel as:
Baptizer with the Holy Spirit
Deliverer
Judge

AMOS

AUTHOR: **Amos**

THEME: **A Coming Judgment for Sin**

CATEGORY: **Minor Prophet**

FASCINATING FACTS

1. Amos carries one of the clearest examples of the constraint of the divine calling to be found anywhere in Scripture (7:14–15).

2. Amos is the only Old Testament prophet who was from one portion of the divided Kingdom and was called to prophesy to the other portion.

3. The book of Amos is one of the clearest and most articulate cries for justice and righteousness in all of the Bible.

4. Amos makes many references and allusions to previous history and to the Pentateuch.

5. The only Old Testament occurrences of the name "Amos" are found here in his book.

6.   Amos, a sheepherder and fruit grower by trade, makes many references to nature and the wilderness (3:4–5; 5:8; etc.).

7.   Amos 9 contains some of the greatest prophecies of Israel's future restoration found anywhere in the Bible.

8.   Amos was the only prophet to state his occupation before asserting his divine calling (7:14).

9.   Amos' familiar statement, "for three transgressions . . . and for four" is repeated seven times in this book.

10. Like many of the unschooled New Testament disciples (Acts 4:13), Amos was called by God into full-time ministry without any formal training.

11. Amos is quoted in the New Testament books of Matthew, Acts, and Romans.

QUOTABLE QUOTES

"It is ever God's way to prepare His servants in secret for the work they are afterwards to accomplish in public. Moses at the backside of the desert; Gideon on the threshing floor; David with his 'few sheep' out upon the hillside; Daniel's refusing to be defiled with the king's meat; John the Baptist in the desert; Peter in his fishing boat; Paul in Arabia; and Amos following the flock and herding the cattle in the wilderness of Tekoa—all alike attest this fact. It is important to observe that only he who has thus learned of God in the school of obscurity is likely to shine in the blaze of publicity."
Harry A. Ironside

"From the obscurity of a shepherd's role Amos stepped out for a few brief moments upon the stage of history, to go down in its annals as one of its first and great reformers."
Homer Hailey

"The book of Amos is one of the most readable, relevant, and moving portions of the Word of God. But in much of church history (until very recent times) little or no attention has been paid to it. Why? It is because the book speaks so powerfully against social injustices and religious formalism, and many who would otherwise read the book have been implicated in such sins and are condemned by it."
James Montgomery Boice

NOTABLE NOTES

In the very first verse of Amos' book, the prophet makes reference to an earthquake, which took place two years later. That earthquake must have been of considerable magnitude and consequence, because the prophet Zechariah refers to it again, some 250 years later (Zechariah 14:5). The Jewish historian Josephus also referred to it in his writings (Antiquities), attributing the cause of the quake to God as a punishment for King Uzziah's usurpation of the temple and priesthood (2 Chronicles 26:16).

CHRIST CONNECTIONS

Christ can be found in Amos as:
Burden-Bearer
Heavenly Bridegroom   **Judge**

OBADIAH

AUTHOR: **Obadiah**

THEME: **The Judgment of Edom**

CATEGORY: **Minor Prophet**

FASCINATING FACTS

1. Obadiah is the shortest and smallest book in the Old Testament, containing just twenty-one verses.

2. Obadiah is never quoted or alluded to in the New Testament.

3. Obadiah is a book with just one theme: the destruction of Edom.

4. The only biblical reference to the prophet Obadiah is found here in the very beginning of this book (1:1).

5. Obadiah was the first prophet to mention the Day of the Lord (verse 15).

6.   Obadiah is the only book in the Old Testament with just a single chapter.

7.   Obadiah was one of the earliest of the writing prophets.

8.   There are at least a dozen other men named "Obadiah" in the Old Testament, but apparently none of them are this prophet (1:1).

9.   The words "Esau" and "Edom" are found nine times in this book.

10. Obadiah illustrates the biblical truth that "pride goes before destruction" (Proverbs 16:18).

QUOTABLE QUOTES

"This is the shortest of all the books of the Old Testament, the least of those tribes, and yet it is not to be passed by or thought meanly of, for this penny has Caesar's image and superscription upon it; it is stamped with a divine authority."
Matthew Henry

"The prophecy of Obadiah is a classic warning against anti-Semitism. The nation that curses and persecutes the Jew will inevitably reap what it sows. The nation that harbors and protects the Jew will surely enjoy the blessing of God."
John Phillips

"One clear light ever burns ahead, leading us upward and onward; it is perfectly expressed in the closing words of Obadiah, 'The kingdom shall be the Lord's.'"
G. Campbell Morgan

NOTABLE NOTES

Obadiah's prophecy was the end result of an ongoing feud that began hundreds of years before that time in the womb of Isaac's wife Rebekah (Genesis 25:20–23). She gave birth to twin boys, Esau and Jacob, whose descendants were bitter rivals throughout the years. Edom, the descendants of Esau, acted very cruelly towards their brethren Israel (Jacob), and it led to their total extinction as a race of people. As God foretold to Abraham, "I will bless those that bless thee, and I will curse those that curse thee" (Genesis 12:3).

CHRIST CONNECTIONS

Christ can be found in Obadiah as:
Savior
Judge
Executor of Divine Retribution

JONAH

AUTHOR: Jonah

THEME: God's Universal Concern for the Lost

CATEGORY: Minor Prophet

FASCINATING FACTS

1. Jonah is one of only two books in the Bible that ends with a question mark (see also: Nahum).

2. Jonah was the only prophet whose ministry was exclusively to the Gentiles.

3. Jonah is the only prophet whose experience Jesus likened to Himself (Matthew 12:40).

4. Jonah was the only prophet who tried to run away from God's commission.

5. Jonah was the only prophet who tried to conceal his message.

6. More than any other Old Testament book, Jonah demonstrates God's compassion and concern for all mankind.

7. Everything and everyone in the book of Jonah obeys the Lord (the storm, the fish, the wind, the Ninevites, the plant, the worm, etc.) except Jonah.

8. Eight hundred years after Jonah fled from Joppa and from his mission to preach to the Gentiles, another Jewish preacher named Peter was commissioned at Joppa to also preach to the Gentiles (Acts 10).

9. There are some ten miracles recorded in this brief book.

10. Some Bible students believe that Jonah actually died inside the great fish and was raised from the dead, making him a more literal type of Christ.

11. Jonah is one of two books in Scripture that has routinely been labeled by nonbelievers as allegorical and not factual (see also: Song of Solomon).

12. The book of Jonah is, in several instances, a recorded conversation between God and this prophet.

13. Jonah is one of only two prophets from the Northern Kingdom of Israel whose writings are found in Scripture (Hosea).

"By picking Jonah from among all of the other available types of death and resurrection with which the Old Testament abounds, Jesus raised the book of Jonah out of the realm of doubt and speculation, above all questions of fiction or parable, and established the book as infallibly inspired, and the events in the book as an actual, literal account of a historic experience and event."
M. R. DeHaan

"If the story of Jonah and the whale is a myth, then so is the story of the resurrection."
John E. Hunter

"The author of the book of Jonah strikes the high-water mark of Old Testament theology. In largeheartedness, in love of mankind, and in the appreciation of the character of God, this little book stands preeminent as the noblest, broadest, and most Christian of all Old Testament literature. It contains one truth far in advance of Jonah's age, a truth which will never pass out of date so long as men have human hearts, and prize the gospel."
George L. Robinson

NOTABLE NOTES

In February of 1891, the whaling ship known as "The Star of the East," was hunting off the Falkland Islands. When a whale was spotted, smaller boats were lowered to harpoon the mammal. One of those smaller boats was capsized, and a sailor named James Bartley disappeared without a trace. After the whale was killed, the crew began the long process of removing the blubber from the whale. The next day, the sailors heard intermittent sounds from the stomach of the whale, and upon cutting the stomach open, discovered their lost sailor! Though initially unconscious, within three weeks he was well enough to return to his ship duties.

CHRIST CONNECTIONS

Christ can be found in Jonah as:
Foreign Missionary
One Greater than Jonah

MICAH

IMPORTANT INFORMATION

AUTHOR: **Micah**

THEME: **Judgment Is Coming**

CATEGORY: **Minor Prophet**

FASCINATING FACTS

1. Micah was the only prophet whose ministry was directed at both kingdoms, Israel and Judah.

2. Micah was the last prophet to speak to the Northern Kingdom (Israel) before its fall.

3. Micah is the only prophet to foretell the actual birthplace of the Messiah, and he did so seven hundred years beforehand.

4. The book of Micah contains several important prophecies within its seven brief chapters.

5. Micah was one of the leading prophets to speak against social injustice, and is oftentimes called "the prophet of the poor."

6. Micah was a contemporary of Isaiah, Hosea, and Amos.

7. Micah bears several similarities to the book of Isaiah, and has been referred to as "a miniature Isaiah" and "Isaiah in shorthand."

8. In Micah, the word "hear" is found some nine times.

9. The book of Micah is considered by many as the most eloquently written of the Minor Prophets.

10. Micah is one of the few prophets referred to by name in the book of another prophet (see Jeremiah 26:18).

QUOTABLE QUOTES

"In Micah's case the message of judgment was heeded, repentance followed, and the disaster was postponed for a century. Hosea and Amos were ignored. Jeremiah was imprisoned. But here was one prophet who was listened to and whose preaching therefore changed history. In coming to Micah we should be encouraged that one man did make a difference."
James Montgomery Boice

"Micah was the first of all the prophets to focus men's eyes upon Bethlehem as the birthplace of a coming Deliverer; a yeoman at that!"
George L. Robinson

"The world will never find its true order and its peace until all other governors—whether emperors, kings, or presidents—have kissed the scepter of the King of kings and reign under His control. That is the great message of Micah."
G. Campbell Morgan

NOTABLE NOTES

Micah is quoted elsewhere in Scripture on three significant occasions. A hundred years after his ministry, his words were quoted by the elders of Judah in Jeremiah 26:18, and as a result, Jeremiah's life was spared! Micah's words were also quoted by the priests and scribes to King Herod in Matthew 2:6, in response to the king's inquiry of where the Messiah was to be born. Finally, Jesus Himself quoted from Micah's words in Matthew 10:35–36 as He sent out His disciples to minister.

CHRIST CONNECTIONS

Christ can be found in Micah as:
Messenger with Beautiful Feet
Rejected King

NAHUM

AUTHOR: Nahum

THEME: Judgment and Destruction of Nineveh

CATEGORY: Minor Prophet

FASCINATING FACTS

1. The book of Nahum picks up where the book of Jonah left off.

2. Nahum is one of two Minor Prophets whose book is devoted exclusively to the story of Nineveh (see also: Jonah).

3. Nahum is never quoted or alluded to in the New Testament.

4. Nahum is one of only two books in the Bible that ends with a question mark (see also: Jonah).

5. There are almost fifty references made to nature in Nahum.

6. Only here does "book" occur in the title of a prophecy (1:1).

7. Nahum not only predicted the demise of the city of Nineveh, but also the manner in which it would fall (1:8).

8.   The only reference to the person of Nahum in the Bible is Nahum 1:1.

9.   Nahum quotes Isaiah in Nahum 1:15, and some believe that Nahum may have been a disciple of Isaiah (Isaiah 8:16).

10. The New Testament city of Capernaum means "city of Nahum," and it is therefore believed by some that Nahum was from the area of Capernaum in Galilee.

11. The book of Nahum is our greatest source of biblical information on the fall of Assyria.

QUOTABLE QUOTES

"The real value, as I see it, of studying a book like Nahum, is that the true wonder of the Bible begins to shine through even those parts of it which seem so utterly at variance with what we have grown to think of as Christian truth."
A. E. Gould

"This little book ranks amongst the finest things in Hebrew literature. In poetic fire and sublimity, it approaches the best work of Isaiah."
G. G. Findlay

"Nahum's mighty intellect, his patriotism and courage, his rare, almost unequaled, gift of vivid presentation, and indeed he looms as one of those outstanding figures in human history who have appeared only at rare intervals."
Walter A. Maier

NOTABLE NOTES

In Nahum 3:11, the prophet predicted that Nineveh would "be hidden." And sure enough, the destruction of Nineveh was so complete that Alexander the Great marched his troops right over the same desolate ground and didn't even realize that there had once been a great city there! It wasn't until 1842 that archaeologists finally discovered the site and location that was once Nineveh.

CHRIST CONNECTIONS

Christ can be found in Nahum as:
Avenger
Stronghold in Day of Trouble
Prophet of Comfort and Vengeance

HABAKKUK

AUTHOR: **Habakkuk**

THEME: **Judgment Against Unrighteousness**

CATEGORY: **Minor Prophet**

FASCINATING FACTS

1. Habakkuk 2:4 is quoted in three different books of the New Testament (Romans, Galatians, and Hebrews).

2. Though a brief book, Habakkuk is quoted or referred to a number of times in the New Testament.

3. The book of Habakkuk is, in its entirety, a recorded conversation between God and this prophet.

4. Habakkuk 3 is recognized as a great psalm of praise, virtually unmatched anywhere else in Scripture.

5. Virtually nothing is known about the prophet Habakkuk except his name, which means "embraced by God."

6. Habakkuk is the only Old Testament prophet who primarily directs his words to God rather than to others.

7. In Habakkuk 2, the prophet utters five "woes" against the Chaldeans.

8. Habakkuk and Jeremiah were the last prophets to speak to the Southern Kingdom of Judah before its captivity by the Babylonians.

9. Habakkuk sees one of the greatest manifestations of God's glory recorded in the Old Testament (3:3–15), reminiscent of Moses at Sinai (Exodus 19) and of Isaiah in the temple (Isaiah 6).

10. From what is recorded in Habakkuk 3:19, we learn that this prophet was involved in temple worship, and therefore, was most likely from the tribe of Levi.

QUOTABLE QUOTES

"Habakkuk is the inspired authority for the fundamental doctrine of justification by faith, and the certainty of judgment to come for those who reject the testimony of the Holy Ghost as to the Lord Jesus Christ."
H. A. Ironside

"When you live by faith, you aren't worried about the things that go on in the world. You may be burdened. It doesn't mean that we shouldn't be concerned about crime and injustice, but we don't lose our faith because of it. We don't become discouraged and despondent and give up. The main message of Habakkuk is that the just shall live by faith."
Warren W. Wiersbe

"It's a beautiful gem of a book written by the prophet who started out wrestling with God and ended up worshipping Him."
Jon Courson

NOTABLE NOTES

Habakkuk 2:4, "But the just shall live by faith," was the biblical doctrine quoted by the apostle Paul in the New Testament books of Romans and Galatians that liberated Martin Luther's heart, turned his life around, and eventually propelled him into the Protestant Reformation. For this reason, Habakkuk has been called "the Grandfather of the Reformation." Those same words from Habakkuk 2:4 also had a profound impact in the life of John Wesley.

CHRIST CONNECTIONS

Christ can be found in Habakkuk as:
God of My Salvation
Judge of Babylon
Rewarder of Those Who Seek Him

IMPORTANT INFORMATION

AUTHOR: **Zephaniah**

THEME: **The Day of the Lord**

CATEGORY: **Minor Prophet**

FASCINATING FACTS

1. Zephaniah was one of the last prophets to warn Judah before her captivity, and is sometimes referred to as "the eleventh-hour prophet."

2. Zephaniah was evidently the great-grandson of King Hezekiah (1:1), and therefore, the only prophet descended from royalty.

3. Zephaniah does something very unusual in his opening words, as he traces his ancestry back four generations.

4. The only reference to the person of Zephaniah in the Bible is Zephaniah 1:1.

5. Zephaniah refers to Jerusalem in such a way as to indicate that the prophet was a resident of the very city he was condemning (1:4, 10).

6. Zephaniah is one of two minor prophets that deal almost exclusively with the coming Day of the Lord (see also: Joel).

7. Zephaniah opens and closes his book by declaring that God was speaking (1:1; 3:20).

8. Zephaniah refers or alludes to the coming Day of the Lord some twenty-three times.

9. Zephaniah's preaching undoubtedly contributed greatly to the reforms in Israel that took place under King Josiah (see 2 Chronicles 34–35).

10. The clearest picture in the Bible of the Day of the Lord was given by Zephaniah.

QUOTABLE QUOTES

"Love seeks the best interests of the beloved. That is what this little book of Zephaniah is all about—the dark side of love...The Father is never more close to you, my friend, then when He is reaching in and taking out of your heart and life those things that offend."
J. Vernon McGee

"Perhaps no prophet gave a more definite declaration of the terrors of the divine judgment against sin than did Zephaniah; this is emphasized by his ignoring utterly the reforms which he saw and knew to be insincere on the part of the people."
G. Campbell Morgan

"No hotter book lies in the Old Testament."
George Adam Smith

NOTABLE NOTES

Zephaniah was a contemporary of the Prophet Jeremiah, and while both men carried similar messages and spoke to the same people and in the same place, their personalities were quite different. Jeremiah was known as the "Weeping Prophet," being sensitive and sympathetic. Zephaniah, on the other hand, was about as straightforward and forthright as any prophet of God. God used both men to help bring renewal and reform in the days of godly King Josiah.

CHRIST CONNECTIONS

Christ can be found in Zephaniah as:
Lord Mighty to Save
Executor of Judgment

HAGGAI

AUTHOR: **Haggai**

THEME: **Putting God First**

CATEGORY: **Minor Prophet**

FASCINATING FACTS

1. Haggai is the only book in the Bible that is two chapters long.

2. Haggai is the second shortest book in the Old Testament (Obadiah is the shortest).

3. Haggai the prophet was a contemporary of Zechariah, and both of them are named in the book of Ezra.

4. Haggai's prophecies are more accurately dated than any others in Scripture.

5. Haggai was the first prophet to be heard after the Babylonian captivity.

6. Haggai's total prophetic ministry lasted less than four months.

7.   Haggai uses the phrases "says the Lord" and "Lord of hosts" a dozen times each.

8.   Haggai's brief prophecy includes at least seven questions.

9.   Haggai was one of just a few prophets who saw immediate results after his preaching—in this case, just twenty-three days later (1:15)!

10. Haggai 2 contains one of the most remarkable prophecies of the coming Messiah (verses 6–9).

11. Haggai is quoted on only one occasion in the New Testament (Hebrews 12:26).

12. The prophet Haggai is the only man in Scripture who bears that name.

QUOTABLE QUOTES

"His [Haggai's] words are all the working out of one idea— the unprofitableness, on the whole and in the long-run, of a godless life." **Alexander Maclaren**

"Haggai himself seems to have almost finished his earthly course, before he was called to be a prophet; and in four months his office was closed...yet in his brief space he first stirred up the people in one month to rebuild the temple." **E. B. Pusey**

"The brief record of Haggai's ministry does...show him as a man of conviction. He has the unique place among the prophets of having really been listened to and his words obeyed...Though his words were plain and not poetic, he had one major point to make; and he made it forcefully and well." Robert L. Alden

NOTABLE NOTES

Haggai the prophet was a contemporary of the Chinese philosopher Confucius. Haggai's ministry was also in close proximity to the spiritual leader Buddha in India, who preached his first sermon within a year after Haggai's prophecy.

CHRIST CONNECTIONS

Christ can be found in Haggai as:
Prophet, Priest, and King
Builder of the House of the Lord

ZECHARIAH

IMPORTANT INFORMATION

AUTHOR: **Zechariah**

THEME: **Israel's Future Blessing**

CATEGORY: **Minor Prophet**

FASCINATING FACTS

1. The name of God as "Lord of Hosts" is found some fifty times in this book.

2. Zechariah is the longest book of the Minor Prophets.

3. Zechariah contains more Messianic prophecies than any other book in the Old Testament except Isaiah.

4. Zechariah is quoted or referred to at least forty times in the New Testament.

5. Zechariah is quoted from or alluded to by other books in Scripture more than any other Old Testament book.

6. Zechariah makes more references and allusions to the coming Messiah than all of the other minor prophets combined.

7. Zechariah saw at least eight different visions in one single night (1:7–6:8).

8. There are at least two dozen men in Scripture who bear the name of Zechariah, including the author of this book.

9. Zechariah uses the phrase "the Word of the Lord" fourteen times.

10. In Zechariah, the city of Jerusalem is named more than forty times.

11. The book of Zechariah has been called "the Apocalypse of the Old Testament."

12. The book of Zechariah contains more references to angels than almost any other book of the Old Testament.

QUOTABLE QUOTES

"The book of Zechariah is the most Messianic, the most truly apocalyptic and eschatological, of all the writings of the Old Testament."
George L. Robinson

"The book of the prophet Zechariah is not much studied nor adequately understood in our day...yet the book as a whole can be studied with great profit and to the strengthening of one's faith. The New Testament makes repeated use of the book. So should we."
H. C. Leupold

"While most Christians are aware of the great messianic prophecies in Isaiah, few are cognizant of the fact that Zechariah is rich with predictions of Christ as well—of both His first and second comings."
Harold L. Willmington

NOTABLE NOTES

The book of Zechariah makes some amazing and important prophecies concerning the Messiah. Some of those Old Testament prophecies are only found in Zechariah, and they include: Christ's triumphal entry into Jerusalem on the back of a donkey (9:9); the betrayal of Christ for thirty pieces of silver (11:12); and the usage of those thirty pieces of betrayal money to purchase a potter's field (11:13).

CHRIST CONNECTIONS

Christ can be found in Zechariah as:
Righteous Branch
Yahweh's Servant
Smitten Shepherd
King-Priest

MALACHI

IMPORTANT INFORMATION

AUTHOR: **Malachi**

THEME: **A Warning to Backsliders**

CATEGORY: **Minor Prophet**

FASCINATING FACTS

1. Along with Obadiah, Malachi is the most obscure Old Testament prophet. His only reference is in 1:1, and it contains no family or geographic history.

2. Malachi was the last prophet to write in the Old Testament.

3. The statement "thus says the Lord of hosts" is recorded some twenty times in Malachi, emphasizing that it was God's message.

4. Malachi lists more questions per verses than any other book of the Bible, with some twenty-seven questions in just fifty-five verses.

5. Malachi is the only prophet who concludes his book with judgment.

6. Malachi, the last book of the Old Testament, and Revelation, the last book of the New Testament, both end with warnings.

7. In Malachi, well over three-quarters of the verses are spoken by God, the highest percentage of all the prophets.

8. Malachi records the most familiar passage on tithing found in the Old Testament (3:8–10).

9. Malachi closes his book with a look backward at Moses and a look forward to Elijah (4:5–6).

10. Malachi lists the last Old Testament Messianic prophecy (4:2).

11. Malachi is the last message from God to His people for 400 years.

12. Portions of Malachi are written in the form of a debate, unlike any other book of the Bible.

13. Malachi is one of the most argumentative books of the Bible.

QUOTABLE QUOTES

"I think that none of the messages of these minor prophets fits the present age as exactly as does this of Malachi."
G. Campbell Morgan

"The more I read this book, the more I see the present generation illustrated in vivid colors. The people concerned were not the heathen or pagan tribes of those days, but the priests and the people of God. The Bible is here showing that before the darkness falls there is dissension, and before the silence there is sacrilege."
John E. Hunter

"God and Malachi wanted a righteous nation, a pure and devoted priesthood, happy homes, God-fearing children, and a people characterized by truth, integrity, generosity, gratitude, fidelity, love, and hope."
Robert L. Alden

NOTABLE NOTES

At the end of Malachi, there is a promise that God will one day send forth Elijah the Prophet (Malachi 4:5). In recognition of that promise, when the Jewish people observe the Passover Seder meal, the door is left ajar, an extra place setting is fixed, and an extra glass of wine is set there. That glass is called "Elijah's cup," and it is set out in anticipation of Elijah's return. In Matthew 17:10–13, Jesus states that Elijah has already come, in the person of John the Baptist. However, many recognize that God also stated that Elijah himself would return just before the Day of the Lord. Therefore, many believe that he will return as one of the two witnesses referenced in Revelation 11.

CHRIST CONNECTIONS

Christ can be found in Malachi as:
Sun of Righteousness
Messenger of the New Covenant
Refiner and Purifier of His people

MATTHEW

AUTHOR: **Matthew**

THEME: **Christ the Messiah-King**

CATEGORY: **Gospel**

FASCINATING FACTS

1. Matthew makes first mention of the "church" in the New Testament (16:18), and makes the only reference to it in the Gospels.

2. Matthew uses the term "King" more times than any other New Testament book.

3. Matthew contains the shortest prayer in the Bible: "Lord, save me!" (14:30).

4. Matthew is one of two Gospels that contain the only recorded earthly conversation between God and Satan in Scripture (chapter 4).

5. Matthew refers to more Old Testament books than any other New Testament book does.

6. Matthew's Gospel contains the most complete record of what Jesus said, with His spoken words found in about sixty percent of its total verses.

7. Nowhere in the four Gospels do we find a single recorded word that Matthew himself spoke.

8. Matthew uses the phrase "the kingdom of heaven" over thirty times in his Gospel, a phrase found nowhere else in the New Testament.

9. Matthew records three miracles by Jesus found nowhere else: the healing of the two blind men (chapter 9), the deliverance of the demon-possessed man (chapter 9), and the coin in the mouth of the fish (chapter 17).

10. Matthew contains one of the only two genealogies of Jesus (chapter 1), and it traces His lineage back to Abraham.

11. Only in Matthew's Gospel do we have the record of the visitation by the Magi to the Christ Child (chapter 2).

12. In Matthew's genealogy of Jesus, there are references to four Old Testament women with tainted pasts: Tamar (harlotry); Rahab (prostitute); Ruth (Moabitess); and Bathsheba (adulteress).

13. The Gospel of Matthew records five major discourses of Jesus.

14. Matthew's Gospel is by far the most Jewish of the four Gospels.

15. Only Matthew refers to himself in Scripture as a "tax collector" (10:3)—the other Gospel writers refer to him as Levi.

QUOTABLE QUOTES

"Matthew was the most widely read gospel in the early church. The patristic writers quoted from it more than from any of the others. It greatly influenced the thinking of early Christians."
D. Edmond Hiebert

"Matthew is the gospel written by a Jew to Jews about a Jew."
Talk Thru The Bible

"No gospel is more instructive to those who are the Lord's disciples and who are called to represent Him in the world. The lessons on discipleship are life-changing for the reader, as they were for the eleven who were Jesus' first followers. Thus, with all its great themes of majesty and glory, rejection and apostasy, the book of Matthew lacks no practicality. Woven through all that is the constant thread of revealed instruction for those who are His representatives among men."
John F. MacArthur Jr.

NOTABLE NOTES

There are several unique dreams recorded in the Gospel of Matthew. In chapter 1, there is Joseph's dream in which an angel explains Mary's pregnancy to him, thereby averting a divorce. In chapter 2, there is Joseph's dream in which an angel warns him to flee from Herod with Mary and the Child into Egypt. Later on, in another dream, an angel tells Joseph that he can return to Israel from Egypt. In the same chapter, in still another dream, God instructs Joseph to relocate to Galilee. Finally, in chapter 27, there is the dream of Pilate's wife, who tells her husband that Jesus is a just Man, and that Pilate should have nothing to do with Him.

CHRIST CONNECTIONS

Christ can be found in Matthew as:
Son of David
Head of the Church
Savior

MARK

IMPORTANT INFORMATION

AUTHOR: **Mark**

THEME: **Christ the Servant**

CATEGORY: **Gospel**

FASCINATING FACTS

1. Mark is the shortest and most graphic of the four Gospels.

2. Mark was the first of the four Gospels to be written.

3. Mark's gospel is one of action, and the word "straightway" (or "immediately") is recorded more than forty times.

4. Mark's gospel records about eighteen of Jesus' many parables.

5. Over one-third of Mark's Gospel focuses on the final eight days of Jesus, from Palm Sunday to Resurrection Sunday.

6. Mark's Gospel contains very few Old Testament references.

7. Mark's Gospel records fewer of Christ's teachings than any of the other three gospels.

8. Only in Mark's Gospel are we told that Jesus was a carpenter (6:3).

9. Because only Mark's Gospel records the story of the young man who fled away naked, many believe that it is a reference to Mark himself.

10. Mark's Gospel records half of Jesus' miracles (eighteen), and he devotes more space, proportionately, to miracles than the other Gospels.

11. Mark's Gospel was written to a Roman audience and mindset, and the last human to speak in this Gospel was the Roman centurion who proclaimed Jesus to be the Son of God (15:39).

12. Mark was not one of the main disciples, and the acceptance of his Gospel account stems from the knowledge that Peter supplied Mark with much of the information used in writing this gospel.

QUOTABLE QUOTES

"There is a freshness about this gospel . . . Here we find rapid action, vivid detail, picturesque language. Many a preacher might be jolted out of his rut—another word for long grave—by letting the impact of Mark really hit him."
Ralph Earle

"This gospel emphasizes what Jesus did rather than what He said."
Charles C. Ryrie

"This gospel has the charm of two personalities who contributed to its contents, Peter and John Mark. Both were vivacious and versatile and have preserved the portrait of Jesus with the freshness of the morning."
A. T. Robertson

NOTABLE NOTES

Since Simon Peter refers to John Mark as "Mark my son" in his first epistle (1 Peter 5:13), many people believe that Mark was converted and discipled under Peter's ministry. If this is true, something else that these two held in common was their well-known moments of failure. Peter's came when he denied the Lord three times (Matthew 26); while Mark's came when he abandoned Paul and Barnabas during their first missionary journey (Acts 13:13). The lives of both men remind us that the Lord is a God of second chances.

CHRIST CONNECTIONS

Christ can be found in Mark as:
Suffering Servant of Yahweh
Mighty King

LUKE

IMPORTANT INFORMATION

AUTHOR: **Luke**

THEME: **The Humanity of Christ**

CATEGORY: **Gospel**

FASCINATING FACTS

1. Luke, the author of this book, is the only known Gentile author of Scripture (Colossians 4:10–14), and wrote more words of the New Testament than anyone else.

2. Luke is the longest Gospel, and the longest book in the New Testament, with 1,151 verses.

3. Luke's account is the most extensive and precise of the four Gospels (1:1–3).

4. Luke and Matthew contain the only recorded earthly conversation between God and Satan in Scripture (chapter 4).

5. Luke's Gospel contains one of just two genealogies of Jesus (chapter 3), and it traces His lineage back to Adam.

6. Luke is the only Gospel that tells us about the salvation of the dying thief who was crucified with Jesus.

7. Luke's Gospel gives us the most complete account of Christ's birth, childhood, and ancestry.

8. Luke's Gospel is the only New Testament book that references the name of Gabriel the angel (1:19, 26), and one of only two books in the Bible that does so (Daniel 8:16).

9. More than one-half of the material in Luke's Gospel is found in no other gospel.

10. Luke has been called "The Gospel of Womanhood" because he emphasizes the role of women, referring to them some forty-three times.

11. Luke's Gospel contains five great hymns or songs and three angelic benedictions (chapters 1–2).

12. Luke's account is the most literary and classical in style and language of the four Gospels.

13. Luke's Gospel uses the phrase "Son of Man" which was Jesus' most commonly used designation for Himself, at least twenty-five times.

14. Luke's Gospel records twenty-two parables, seventeen of which are found only in his account.

15. Luke was a physician (Colossians 4:14); therefore, he uses many medical terms in his writing.

16. Luke's Gospel is the most socially minded of the four Gospels, with more recorded instances of Jesus' dealings with the poor, strangers, and so on.

17. Unlike the other Gospel writers, Luke places emphasis upon the activity of the Holy Spirit in the ministry of Jesus.

18. Luke's gospel emphasizes prayer (1:10; 3:21; 9:29; 23:46; etc.).

QUOTABLE QUOTES

"There is no gospel which more shows the mind and love of God than this of Luke. None is more truly and evidently inspired. Nevertheless there is none so deeply marked by traces of the human hand and heart."
William Kelly

"There is something especially attractive about this Gospel."
Donald Guthrie

"The message of this Gospel is not a simple message. The more carefully we study this book the more we are impressed with its profundity, with the wonder and spaciousness of the thing it has to say to us concerning Christ . . . What is the message of this Gospel to the world? Carry it to the ends of the earth, let it speak its own truth to the men who are lost, and it tells them of a Kinsman Who, to borrow the old Hebrew figure, is able to discharge their debt, destroy their enemies, make possible the redemption of their persons, and the redemption of their inheritance, as offspring of God."
G. Campbell Morgan

NOTABLE NOTES

A very old tradition dating back to the sixth century asserts that Luke was a painter and that he painted a portrait of Mary, the mother of Jesus. Certainly, Luke painted beautiful pictures with his words. His account is viewed as being by far the best literary work of the four Gospels. This is evidenced by the instance when French rationalistic critic and notorious nonbeliever Ernest Renan once said that Luke's Gospel was "the most beautiful book ever written."

CHRIST CONNECTIONS

Christ can be found in Luke as:
Son of Man
Sympathetic High Priest
Savior

JOHN

IMPORTANT INFORMATION

AUTHOR: John the Apostle

THEME: The Deity of Christ

CATEGORY: Gospel

FASCINATING FACTS

1. John's Gospel contains the shortest verse in the Bible, "Jesus wept," in John 11:35.

2. The names "Jesus" and "Christ" appear more times here (over 170) than in any other book of the Bible.

3. John's Gospel contains the longest prayer of the New Testament: John 17.

4. One-third of John's Gospel is a record of the last eight days of Christ's life before His death, from Palm Sunday to Easter Sunday.

5. John is the most theological of the four Gospels.

6. John's Gospel contains no parables and only eight miracles, five of which are not recorded in the other Gospels.

7. John 3:16 is undoubtedly the most quoted and most familiar verse in all of Scripture.

8. In John's Gospel, the word "believe" appears some one hundred times, emphasizing the gospel message.

9. John's Gospel presents the strongest evidence for the deity of Jesus Christ.

10. Over ninety percent of John's Gospel is unique from the other three synoptic Gospels.

11. Only John's Gospel contains Jesus' "I am" statements that speak of His being the Messiah.

12. John begins his Gospel with the same language of Genesis: "In the beginning."

QUOTABLE QUOTES

"The Gospel of John is the most influential Book that has ever come from the pen of any man."
Philip Schaff

"This is the Gospel of the Divine Life of Jesus. The eagle has always been its recognized emblem, as denoting its sublime and heavenly character. And, clearly, in its dictation, its insights into the deepest truths, its repeated testimony to the Glory and Deity of our Lord, it holds a unique place among the records of His life."
F. B. Meyer

"No Gospel of the New Testament is more greatly loved than the Gospel of John. Among young and old alike its profound message, beautiful imagery, and simple language have won their way into countless hearts."
Homer A. Kent Jr.

NOTABLE NOTES

The oldest surviving New Testament text that we have is a fragment of John 18:31–33, 37–38, which includes Pilate's question to Jesus: "Are You the King of the Jews?" That fragment dates to about A.D. 125, roughly one generation after the original was written. It is located in the John Rylands Library in Manchester, England.

CHRIST CONNECTIONS

Christ can be found in John as:
Son of God
One Who Brings Eternal Life

ACTS

AUTHOR: **Luke**

THEME: **History and Life of the Early Church**

CATEGORY: **History**

FASCINATING FACTS

1. Acts is the most historical book of the New Testament.

2. Without the book of Acts, we would have very little background information on many of the other New Testament epistles and churches.

3. The Holy Spirit is mentioned over fifty times in Acts, more than any other New Testament book.

4. Acts records the birth of the church (Acts 2).

5. Acts is the only unfinished book in the Bible, as the history of the church still continues to this day.

6.   Acts records many church firsts, such as the first martyrs, the first deacons, the first pastors, the first missionaries, and the first Gentile converts.

7.   Almost every chapter in Acts refers to prayer, and every chapter shows the result of prayer.

8.   Luke, the author of this book, is the only known Gentile author of Scripture.

9.   Acts contains the longest recorded sermon in the New Testament, preached by Stephen in chapter 7.

10. In Acts, believers are called "Christians" for the first time (11:26).

11. In Acts, we have the last two biblical resurrections of identified people: Dorcas (9:40–41) and Eutychus (20:9–12).

12. In Acts, Luke makes references to more than one hundred people, and to approximately eighty locations.

13. Acts, with its three major missionary journeys, has been called the greatest missionary story ever told.

14. In the New Testament, there are four resurrections recorded by Luke, two in his Gospel and two in the book of Acts.

QUOTABLE QUOTES

"It is no exaggeration to say that the book of Acts is one of the most graphic pieces of writing in all literature...Acts is a dawn, a glorious sunrise, a bursting forth in a dark world of eternal light; it is a Book precious beyond all price."
W. Graham Scroggie

"No book of the New Testament is more appealing as it beckons the church of today to look at the church as it was at the beginning...It is thrilling narrative, striking characterization, and dynamic achievement."
Ralph G. Turnbull

"The story of the church which unfolds in the Acts of the Apostles is one of the most fascinating stories of the Bible. It is the story of young churches in action—not in meditation, contemplation or worship—but action. In fact, action is the theme as well as the name of the book of Acts. It is its atmosphere, story, movement, and inspiration."
Roy Laurin

NOTABLE NOTES

On the day of Pentecost, as Peter preached the gospel, some 3,000 people were saved. In contrast, after the golden calf tragedy at Mt. Sinai, some 3,000 people lost their lives. Consequently, when the Law was first given at Mt. Sinai, 3,000 souls died—and when grace was first preached in the church on Pentecost, 3,000 souls were saved. The Law kills, but grace saves!

CHRIST CONNECTIONS

Christ can be found in Acts as:
One Sitting at the Right Hand of God
Prince of the Kings of the Earth

ROMANS

IMPORTANT INFORMATION

AUTHOR: **Paul**

THEME: **Salvation by Grace Through Faith**

CATEGORY: **Pauline Epistle**

FASCINATING FACTS

1. In Romans, Paul quotes more from the Old Testament (especially from Isaiah and Psalms) than in all of his other epistles combined.

2. In Romans, just about every major doctrine of the Christian faith is put forth.

3. Romans is one of only two epistles in which Paul includes several personal and individual greetings (see also: Colossians), and in both cases, he had not visited either church previously.

4. The epistle of Romans is Paul's most formal and systematic writing.

5. In Romans, there are well over 200 words not found in any of Paul's other writings; and nearly 100 of those words are unique to the New Testament

6. Although Romans is Paul's second largest epistle (see 1 Corinthians), it is his most important work.

7. Romans is the first of three New Testament books to quote Habakkuk 2:4 (see also: Galatians and Hebrews).

8. In Romans, three key words appear numerous times: "law" (78 times), "righteousness" (66 times), and "faith" (62 times).

9. In Romans, Paul makes reference to many Old Testament figures, including Adam, Abraham, Sarah, Jacob, Esau, Rebekah, David, and others.

10. Romans 16 contains Paul's most eloquent benediction (16:25–27).

11. Many scholars believe that the epistle to the Romans was hand-delivered by Phoebe, the faithful sister that Paul describes in chapter 16.

12. Romans is so foundational to the faith that it has been called the "Constitution of Christianity."

QUOTABLE QUOTES

"This epistle is the chief part of the New Testament, and the very purest Gospel . . . It can never be read or considered too much or too well; and the more it is handled, the more precious it becomes, and the better it tastes."
Martin Luther

"It opened the door to all of the treasures in Scripture."
John Calvin

"It is the greatest and richest of all the apostolic works."
F. B. Meyer

"This epistle has ever been considered as St. Paul's masterpiece, whether judged from an intellectual or theological standpoint, and the greatest of men have ever valued it most highly."
Robert Lee

NOTABLE NOTES

John Chrysostom had this epistle read to him once a week for eighteen years. Martyn Lloyd-Jones, the great expositor of Scripture, spent fourteen years teaching through the book of Romans and yet never finished his series before he resigned from his church. Donald Grey Barnhouse broadcast weekly messages through Romans for eleven years on the radio. Several hundred years ago, one church leader copied the entire book of Romans by hand—twice—in order to become more familiar with it. Early church father Augustine was converted by reading Romans. It propelled Martin Luther into the Protestant Reformation. And, it inspired John Wesley into the great Wesleyan Revival of England.

CHRIST CONNECTIONS

Christ can be found in Romans as:
Lord Our Righteousness
Justifier, Redeemer, and Savior

1 CORINTHIANS

IMPORTANT INFORMATION

AUTHOR: Paul

THEME: Correcting a Carnal Church

CATEGORY: Pauline Epistle

FASCINATING FACTS

1. 1 Corinthians is the longest of Paul's epistles.

2. 1 and 2 Corinthians are, by content, Paul's most practical epistles.

3. In 1 Corinthians, Paul uses the title "The Lord Jesus Christ" six times in just the first ten verses, emphasizing Christ's Lordship.

4. 1 Corinthians is an epistle of reproof and correction.

5. 1 Corinthians addresses practically every existing church problem.

6. 1 Corinthians contains the most extensive treatment of spiritual gifts found anywhere in the New Testament.

7. 1 Corinthians provides us one of the most vivid windows into the life of the early church.

8. In 1 Corinthians 15, we find the greatest and earliest New Testament discourse on the Resurrection.

9. The church at Corinth was the least spiritual of all the churches addressed by letter in the New Testament.

10. In 1 Corinthians, there are more than 230 words not used in any of Paul's other writings, and 100 of those words are unique to the New Testament.

11. 1 Corinthians contains one of our earliest references to the Lord's Supper, found in chapter 11.

QUOTABLE QUOTES

"This Letter is addressed not just to a few people in Corinth, a city that is now in ruins, but to the church of Jesus Christ in any city of the world in any era of history, even the times in which we live."
Alan Redpath

"1 Corinthians is so vital to us. Conditions have not changed much. Many of the problems that confronted the Corinthians plague present-day believers as well. Living wisely for God is not easy in the midst of a sinful and materialistic age. But 1 Corinthians is filled with valuable and important lessons...which [are] so essential for our walk with the Lord."
J. Allen Blair

"These epistles [Corinthians] . . . in reference to all practical measures in the establishment of the church among the heathen, and in its conduct in Christian lands, are among the most important portions of the word of God."
Charles Hodge

NOTABLE NOTES

According to 1 Corinthians 5:9, 11, Paul had written an earlier letter to the church at Corinth, which has since been lost. Also, 2 Corinthians 2:4 points to still another letter not found today. Therefore, 1 and 2 Corinthians are actually Paul's second and fourth letters to that church. Consequently, it makes the church at Corinth the only known church to which Paul ever sent four letters.

CHRIST CONNECTIONS

Christ can be found in 1 Corinthians as:
Foundation of the Church
Unifier
Great Sacrifice
Resurrected One
Coming Lord

2 CORINTHIANS

AUTHOR: **Paul**

THEME: **The Ministry of the Church**

CATEGORY: **Pauline Epistle**

FASCINATING FACTS

1. 2 Corinthians is the most autobiographical of all of Paul's epistles.

2. In 2 Corinthians, different forms of the word "ministry" are used some eighteen times, underscoring the epistle's theme.

3. 1 and 2 Corinthians are perhaps Paul's most practical epistles.

4. 2 Corinthians is one of Paul's least doctrinal letters.

5. The church at Corinth was the least spiritual of all the churches addressed by letter in the New Testament.

6. 2 Corinthians is the least systematic of all of Paul's epistles.

7. In 2 Corinthians, there are at least 170 words that Paul does not use anywhere else, and at least 90 of those words are unique to the New Testament.

8. In 2 Corinthians chapters 8 and 9, we find the longest New Testament passage on the subject of giving.

9. In 2 Corinthians, Paul's companion and helper Titus is referred to by name no less than nine times, far more than anyone else.

10. In 2 Corinthians, the person and the ministry of Satan are emphasized (4:4; 11:14; etc.).

QUOTABLE QUOTES

"Nowhere does Paul open his heart to his readers so completely as he does in his second letter [to the Corinthians] as he relates some of God's dealings with him in his inner life."
Alan Redpath

"The two [epistles of Corinthians] together are valuable beyond all estimate for an understanding of the problems of first-century Christians, and for an appreciation of the greatest missionary of the Christian era."
W. Graham Scroggie

"This book reveals the warm, human character of Paul. Many have pictured Paul as the methodical logician of Romans or Galatians...This epistle, however, is emotional, full of tears and grief. It was written more with the heart than with the head."
Robert G. Gromacki

In chapter 12 of this epistle, the apostle Paul briefly describes his experience of being caught up into the third heaven, or Paradise. Paul states that he heard things there that are unlawful for a man to speak. Many commentators believe that this unusual experience in Paul's ministry took place when he was stoned and left for dead by a mob in the city of Lystra (see Acts 14:19).

CHRIST CONNECTIONS

Christ can be found in 2 Corinthians as:
Son of God
One Who Anoints
Reconciler

GALATIANS

IMPORTANT INFORMATION

AUTHOR: **Paul**

THEME: **Justification by Faith**

CATEGORY: **Pauline Epistle**

FASCINATING FACTS

1. Galatians was most likely the first epistle that Paul wrote.

2. Galatians is Paul's only letter that was addressed to a group of churches (1:2).

3. It is the only epistle of Paul's that does not begin with a word of thanksgiving and praise, and it is the apostle's most severe letter.

4. In Galatians, Paul makes no request for prayer from these believers, which was very unusual.

5. In Galatians, Paul emphasizes the doctrine of justification by faith more than in any of his other epistles, including Romans.

6. Galatians is Paul's only epistle in which he draws attention to his handwriting (6:11).

7. Only in Galatians do we learn of a three-year period shortly after Paul's conversion in which he went into the deserts of Arabia (1:17).

8. Galatians is undoubtedly Paul's most passionate and emotionally charged epistle.

9. In Galatians, there are some forty-seven references made to Christ.

10. In Galatians, two key words are: law (appears 32 times) and faith (appears 21 times).

11. Galatians 5 contains the well-known and very important passage on the fruit of the Spirit (5:22–23).

QUOTABLE QUOTES

"The epistle to the Galatians is my epistle. I have betrothed myself to it. It is my wife."
Martin Luther

"It is a stern, severe, and solemn message...It has been called the Magna Charta of the early church, the manifesto of Christian liberty, the impregnable citadel, and a veritable Gibraltar against any attack on the heart of the gospel."
J. Vernon McGee

"Paul's letters are probably the most extraordinary letters in the world, but none of them is more remarkable than Galatians. Its vigor, variety, audacity, and self-revealing frankness, together with its deep and direct insight into religious truth, put it in a class by itself among the books of the New Testament."
Edgar J. Goodspeed

NOTABLE NOTES

In Galatians 1:15–16, Paul refers to the fact that he was set apart in his mother's womb for the service to which God had called him. In this regard, we are reminded of the Old Testament prophet Jeremiah, who also stated that he was set apart for God's special calling prior to his birth (see Jeremiah 1:5). Jeremiah even states that God knew him before he was conceived within the womb!

CHRIST CONNECTIONS

Christ can be found in Galatians as:

Great Redeemer

Seed of Abraham

Liberator

EPHESIANS

IMPORTANT INFORMATION

AUTHOR: **Paul**

THEME: **A Walk Worthy of Our Calling**

CATEGORY: **Pauline Epistle**

FASCINATING FACTS

1. The church at Ephesus is the only church to receive a letter from more than one New Testament writer, as John also addressed them (see Revelation 2:1–7).

2. Ephesians is one of Paul's four prison epistles, along with Colossians, Philippians, and Philemon.

3. The church at Ephesus had many well-known preachers, including Paul, Apollos, Timothy, and John.

4. In Ephesians, over one-half of all the verses are repeated in Colossians with some slight variations (the "Twin Epistles").

5. In Ephesians 5, we have the most beautiful New Testament picture of the Christian husband-wife, marriage relationship.

6. Ephesians 6 gives us a detailed teaching on spiritual warfare, including the armor of God.

7. Ephesians 1:3–14 constitutes the longest continuous sentence found anywhere in Scripture, as translated from the Greek.

8. The phrase "in the heavenly places" is found five times in Ephesians, but nowhere else in the New Testament (1:3, 20; 2:6; 3:10; 6:12).

9. In Ephesians, the personality of the Holy Spirit is emphasized throughout this epistle (1:13; 2:18; 3:5; 4:30; 5:18; 6:17).

10. In Ephesians, there are no personal greetings, despite the fact that Paul had been to Ephesus twice, staying for three years on the second visit.

11. In Ephesians, the word "grace," one of the key words, is used some twelve times.

12. In Ephesians, the terms "in Christ" and "in Him" are used fifteen times.

QUOTABLE QUOTES

"It is the epistle of the Heavenlies, a solemn liturgy, an ode to Christ and His spotless bride, the Song of Songs in the New Testament."
Philip Schaff

"The whole letter is a magnificent combination of Christian doctrine and Christian duty, Christian faith and Christian life, what God has done through Christ and what we must be and do in consequence."
John R. W. Stott

"Of all God's wonders in His natural creation, which He has given me to see, none seems more wonderful than the Grand Canyon...Ephesians is the Grand Canyon of Scripture."
Ruth Paxson

"Ephesians—carefully, reverently, prayerfully considered— will change our lives. It is not so much a question of what we will do with the epistle, but what it will do with us."
R. Kent Hughes

NOTABLE NOTES

The church at Ephesus cross-sectioned the lives of many well-known New Testament figures. Paul went there with Priscilla and Aquila on his second missionary journey (see Acts 18). Apollos and Timothy were both involved there (see Acts18; 1 Timothy 1). Tradition says that after Paul died, John made his headquarters there, and then eventually died there. Tradition also states that Mary, the mother of Jesus, died and was buried there.

CHRIST CONNECTIONS

Christ can be found in Ephesians as:
Heavenly King
Reconciler
Head of the Body
Giver of Ministry Gifts

PHILIPPIANS

IMPORTANT INFORMATION

AUTHOR: **Paul**

THEME: **Joy in the Midst of All Circumstances**

CATEGORY: **Pauline Epistle**

FASCINATING FACTS

1. Philippians is Paul's warmest and most affectionate epistle.

2. In Philippians, the words "joy" and "rejoice" occur sixteen times and are found in every chapter.

3. Philippians contains one of the most magnificent New Testament passages on the deity and ministry of Christ (2:5–11).

4. Philippians contains no quotations from the Old Testament.

5. The church at Philippi was Paul's most faithful and loyal source of financial support (4:10).

6. The church work at Philippi began with Paul going to jail (Acts 16:25); and this epistle was written by Paul while in jail (Philippians 1:14).

7. Philippians is Paul's only epistle in which he makes reference to church officers in his opening greetings (1:1).

8. Philippians, along with Philemon, are Paul's two most personal letters.

9. Philippians 4:6–8 offers one of the most practical explanations and applications for prayer found anywhere in Scripture.

10. In Philippians 4:4–14, Paul shares a very significant autobiographical sketch of himself.

11. Only in Philippians and Thessalonians does Paul not begin with a declaration of his apostleship.

12. Philippians is one of Paul's four "prison epistles," along with Ephesians, Colossians, and Philemon.

QUOTABLE QUOTES

"Paul's Letter to the Philippians is like an open window into the Apostle's very heart. In it we have the artless outpouring of his unrestrained love for and his unallayed joy in his devoted and loyal Philippian friends. It is the most intimate and spontaneous of his writings."
D. Edmond Hiebert

"This is an epistle of the heart, a true love letter, full of friendship, gratitude, and confidence."
George G. Findlay

"Joy is the music that runs through this epistle, the sunshine that spreads all over it. The whole epistle radiates joy and happiness."
R. C. H. Lenski

"The Epistle to the Philippians has no doctrines to expound. It has no errors to correct; no issues to refute. It has a living Christ to introduce and commend to human need. Not a Christ disassociated from life's living, but a Christ experienced and proved in the utmost stress of life."
Norman B. Harrison

NOTABLE NOTES

The church at Philippi was the first church founded in Europe (see Acts 16). This church work began with the conversion of a woman named Lydia who had been meeting regularly outside of the city, beside a river, for prayer along with other women (see Acts 16:13–15). Other women converts also became prominent within the church (Philippians 4:2–3). This corresponds with the fact that women were held in higher regard in this province of Macedonia. Paul's greatest satanic challenge even came in the form of a demon-possessed girl.

CHRIST CONNECTIONS

Christ can be found in Philippians as:
Source of the Fruits of Righteousness
One Equal with God Who Humbled Himself
Coming One

COLOSSIANS

IMPORTANT INFORMATION

AUTHOR: **Paul**

THEME: **Complete in Christ**

CATEGORY: **Pauline Epistle**

FASCINATING FACTS

1. Colossians is one of only two of Paul's epistles written to a church that he had never previously visited (Romans).

2. Colossians, like Philippians, contains some of the greatest passages on the deity and ministry of Christ (1:15–20; 2:9–10).

3. Colossians contains one of Paul's briefest benedictions (4:18).

4. Over four-fifths of the verses here in Colossians are repeated in Ephesians with some slight variations.

5. In Colossians, Paul dealt with many forms of false teaching and harmful doctrines, including legalism, mysticism, asceticism, and Gnosticism.

6. Though Colossians is a smaller epistle, Paul uses some fifty-five words that are not found in any of his other epistles.

7. There are no references made in Colossians to the Old Testament.

8. Colossians is one of the most Christ-centered books in the Bible.

9. Though the Epistle to the Colossians is very important, the city of Colosse itself was by far the least important city to which Paul had ever sent a letter, and afterward, the church disappears from Christian history.

10. Colossians contains many unique titles for Christ, such as "image of the invisible God" (1:15), "firstborn from the dead" (1:18), and so on.

11. Colossians is one of Paul's four prison epistles, along with Ephesians, Philippians, and Philemon.

QUOTABLE QUOTES

"The Epistle to the Colossians contains the heart of the Christian message. One cannot engage in a serious study of its contents without being deeply and profoundly affected...No other New Testament book is more relevant in our generation, for the manifestations of the heresy at Colosse are present today."
Charles N. Pickell

"The Epistle to the Colossians is a short one, but tremendous in its depth and height, its scope and grasp."
A. T. Robertson

"As therefore this Epistle forms one of the peaks in the New Testament revelation of Christ, all who desire to reach a correct understanding of His Person

must resolve to scale its heights. The message of Colossians is that believers are complete in Christ."
Geoffrey B. Wilson

NOTABLE NOTES

Epaphras, the pastor and probable founder of the church at Colosse, traveled well over 1,000 miles—from Colosse to Rome—just to seek Paul's counsel and help for handling serious doctrinal attacks against the Christian faith in that region. The epistle to the Colossians is Paul's answer to Epaphras' plea for help. Paul's epistle did not come back with Epaphras, either because he himself was imprisoned with Paul (Philemon 23), or because Paul had asked Epaphras to stay and help him there.

CHRIST CONNECTIONS

Christ can be found in Colossians as:
Preeminent One
Redeemer in the Image of God

1 THESSALONIANS

IMPORTANT INFORMATION

AUTHOR: **Paul**

THEME: **Living in Light of Christ's Return**

CATEGORY: **Pauline Epistle**

FASCINATING FACTS

1. Every chapter in 1 Thessalonians ends with a reference to Christ's return (1:10; 2:19; 3:13; 4:16; and 5:23).

2. This was probably the second epistle written by the apostle Paul, and one of the earliest of the New Testament books.

3. 1 Thessalonians contains the earliest New Testament reference to the Rapture of the Church (4:16).

4. 1 Thessalonians does not contain any quotations from the Old Testament.

5. 1 Thessalonians contains the earliest reference to the trichotomy of our human nature; that we are spirit, soul, and body (5:23).

6. This epistle, along with 2 Thessalonians, has more to do with last-days teaching than any of Paul's other writings.

7. The church at Thessalonica was perhaps the youngest church to which Paul ever wrote, being a year or less old in the Lord.

8. Between 1 and 2 Thessalonians, almost every major doctrine of the Christian faith is mentioned.

9. One out of every four verses in 1 and 2 Thessalonians concerns the fact of Christ's return.

10. In 1 Thessalonians, there are seventeen Greek words not found elsewhere in the New Testament, and another seventeen words that are unique within Paul's epistles.

11. Only in Thessalonians and Philippians does Paul not begin with a declaration of his apostleship.

QUOTABLE QUOTES

"On the subject of the Second Coming, Paul assures the Thessalonians what will happen, but not when it will happen. His discussion throughout is dominated by an emphasis on practical living, rather than on speculation. The best way to prepare for Christ's return is to live faithfully and obediently now."
Nelson's Bible Dictionary

"This Letter, more than any other of Paul's, is characterized by simplicity, gentleness, and affection."
W. Graham Scroggie

"The Epistles [of 1 and 2 Thessalonians] are like finely cut gems. They reflect the depths of theological thought, especially in the area of future things... They are a joy to read and a delight to study."
Charles C. Ryrie

NOTABLE NOTES

Of all of the churches that the apostle Paul established, only six of them ever received letters from him, and only two of them—the church at Corinth and this church at Thessalonica—would ever receive multiple letters. Timothy is the only person to receive two letters from Paul.

CHRIST CONNECTIONS

Christ can be found in 1 Thessalonians as:
Risen Lord
Coming King

2 THESSALONIANS

IMPORTANT INFORMATION

AUTHOR: **Paul**

THEME: **The Second Coming of Christ**

CATEGORY: **Pauline Epistle**

FASCINATING FACTS

1. 2 Thessalonians contains one of the main New Testament teachings concerning the Antichrist (2:3–12).

2. 2 Thessalonians is Paul's shortest letter to a church, and his second shortest epistle overall (see also: Philemon).

3. Eleven times in this short epistle, Paul refers to the "Lord Jesus Christ" as he exhorts these young believers to focus on Him.

4. 2 Thessalonians 2 contains three different titles for the Antichrist: "man of sin" (verse 2), "son of perdition" (verse 2), and "lawless one" (verse 8).

5. In 2 Thessalonians 2, the sinner's condemnation is everlasting (verse 9), and the saint's consolation is everlasting (verse 16).

6. Only in Thessalonians and Philippians does Paul not begin with a declaration of his apostleship.

7. This epistle, along with 1 Thessalonians, has more to do with last-days teaching than any other of Paul's writings.

8. The church at Thessalonica was perhaps the youngest church to which Paul ever wrote, being a year or less old in the Lord.

9. One out of every four verses in 1 and 2 Thessalonians concerns the fact of Christ's return.

10. Between 1 and 2 Thessalonians, almost every major doctrine of the Christian faith is mentioned.

QUOTABLE QUOTES

"Second Thessalonians is a sequel to Paul's letter to the church at Thessalonica. Sequels, at least with regard to books and movies, rarely have quite the punch of the original. However, one look at Paul's closing remarks in 2 Thessalonians...dispels that conclusion with the swiftness of a left jab and the impact of an upper cut."
Charles R. Swindoll

"A wonderful epistle which teaches that the knowledge of prophecy, rather than leading to fanaticism or laziness, brings peace to the heart."
J. Vernon McGee

"I am greatly encouraged that the apostle Paul had to write a second letter to the Thessalonians to explain his first! I have had to do that on occasion."
Ray C. Stedman

In the New Testament, there are nearly 320 references dealing with the subject of Christ's return, or one in every twenty-five verses. In 1 and 2 Thessalonians, that rate jumps dramatically to one in every four verses. More space is dedicated to the subject of Christ's return in the New Testament than to baptism and Communion combined.

CHRIST CONNECTIONS

Christ can be found in 2 Thessalonians as:
Coming King
Great Judge
Faithful One

1 TIMOTHY

IMPORTANT INFORMATION

AUTHOR: **Paul**

THEME: **Proper Church Conduct**

CATEGORY: **Pauline Epistle**

FASCINATING FACTS

1. Timothy is one of only three individuals to whom Paul addressed his epistles, rather than to congregations (see also: Titus and Philemon).

2. 1 Timothy is one of only three Pastoral Epistles, specifically addressing the pastoral care of churches (2 Timothy and Titus).

3. 1 Timothy is the first New Testament book to give detailed instruction for how the church should operate.

4. Timothy is the only person in the New Testament to be called "man of God" (6:11).

5. 1 Timothy contains Paul's shortest benediction (6:21b).

6.   Only in the Pastoral Epistles (1 and 2 Timothy, Titus) did Paul add the word "mercy" to his normal greeting of "grace and peace."

7.   Only in 1 Timothy and Titus do we have a detailed description of the qualifications for church leadership (3:1–13).

8.   Timothy's name appears in the greetings of Paul's epistles more often than any other person's.

9.   The unique phrase of Paul, "this is a faithful saying," is found only five times and only in the Pastoral Epistles, three of those instances being in 1 Timothy (1:15; 3:1; 4:9).

10. In 1 Timothy, the words "doctrine" and "godliness" appear eight times each, tying in with the theme of proper church conduct.

QUOTABLE QUOTES

"The importance of these Pastoral Epistles lies especially in the instruction they give on character, testimony, and care of local churches, God's lamps of witness in a world of darkness."
Homer A. Kent Jr.

"While the epistle is written to a particular person, and to meet peculiar circumstances, it yet has such wide application to ourselves."
Guy H. King

"These [pastoral] epistles are the only part of the New Testament which deals with church problems from an administrative rather than a theological viewpoint."
W. E. Vine

Out of the city of Lystra came perhaps the apostle Paul's most difficult circumstance and his most delightful companion. On Paul's first missionary journey through Lystra, he was stoned by an angry mob, dragged out of the city, and left for dead. However, a young man named Timothy came to faith as a result of Paul's preaching. On Paul's second missionary journey through Lystra, Timothy became Paul's missionary companion. Timothy went on to become like a son to Paul, and he was a constant and faithful companion to the great apostle.

CHRIST CONNECTIONS

Christ can be found in 1 Timothy as:
Enabler Who Ministers
Mediator
God in the Flesh
King of Kings

2 TIMOTHY

IMPORTANT INFORMATION

AUTHOR: **Paul**

THEME: **Carrying on the Ministry**

CATEGORY: **Pauline Epistle**

FASCINATING FACTS

1. 2 Timothy was Paul's final epistle and his last written words before his death.

2. 2 Timothy contains one of the two main statements on the inspiration of Scripture in 2 Timothy 3:16 (see also: 2 Peter 1:20–21).

3. 2 Timothy is one of only three Pastoral Epistles, specifically addressing the pastoral care of churches (see also: 1 Timothy and Titus).

4. 2 Timothy is Paul's only Pastoral Epistle written from prison.

5. Only in the Pastoral Epistles (1 and 2 Timothy, Titus) did Paul add the word "mercy" to his normal greeting of "grace and peace."

6. 2 Timothy contains some twenty-five essential directives from Paul to Timothy.

7. Timothy was one of only three individuals to whom Paul addressed his epistles, rather than to congregations (see also: Titus and Philemon).

8. Though 2 Timothy contains only eighty-three verses in its four brief chapters, it records the names of some twenty-three different people.

9. Only in 2 Timothy do we learn of the names of Timothy's mother and grandmother (1:5), as well as the names of the magicians who opposed Moses in Egypt (3:8).

10. In 2 Timothy 2, Paul uses many metaphors for the faithful Christian: soldier (verse 3), athlete (verse 5), farmer (verse 6), worker (verse 15), and so forth.

QUOTABLE QUOTES

"I have often found it difficult deliberately to read these short chapters through, without finding something like a mist gathering in the eyes. The Writer's heart beats in the writing."
H. C. G. Moule

"It is in a sense the last will and testament of the greatest missionary-theologian of early Christianity."
Robert H. Mounce

"Let us read, let us listen, let us believe. We shall find the dying Letter full of living messages, carried to us by a sure messenger's hand, direct from Him."
H. C. G. Moule

NOTABLE NOTES

Though his death is not recorded in the pages of Scripture, tradition states that the apostle Paul was martyred under the cruel hand of the Roman Emperor, Nero. Tradition affirms that Paul was beheaded on the Ostian Way, west of Rome.

CHRIST CONNECTIONS

Christ can be found in 2 Timothy as:
Victor Over Death
Resurrected Seed of David

TITUS

IMPORTANT INFORMATION

AUTHOR: **Paul**

THEME: **Setting the Church in Order**

CATEGORY: **Pauline Epistle**

FASCINATING FACTS

1. Titus is one of only three individuals to whom Paul wrote; the others were Timothy and Philemon.

2. Titus is one of only three Pastoral Epistles, specifically addressing pastoral care of churches; the others were 1 and 2 Timothy.

3. Only in the Pastoral Epistles (1 and 2 Timothy, Titus) did Paul add the word "mercy" to his normal greeting of "grace and peace."

4. Only in Titus and 1 Timothy do we have a detailed description of the qualifications for church leadership (1:6–9).

5. In Titus, a heavy emphasis is placed upon the importance of good works in the lives of believers (1:16; 2:7, 14; 3:1, 8, 14).

6.   In Titus 1:12, Paul quotes the Cretan poet, Epimenides.

7.   Though Titus is a brief epistle, there are several references made to the key doctrines of the Christian faith.

8.   Though closely associated with the apostle Paul and his missionary work, Titus is never mentioned in the book of Acts.

9.   Titus was one of only two young men that Paul referred to as being his true sons in the faith, the other being Timothy (Titus 1:4; 1 Timothy 1:2).

10.   Titus is the only epistle written to an island location (Crete).

QUOTABLE QUOTES

"This is a short epistle, but yet such a model of Christian doctrine, and composed in such a masterly manner, that it contains all that is needful for Christian knowledge and life."
Martin Luther

"Somehow, as we ponder this short but weighty note to Titus, we have an uneasy feeling that all too many of us modern Christians live far below its simply worded but searching standards...We have much need to linger often among the purifying paragraphs of this little letter."
J. Sidlow Baxter

"The Pastoral Epistles are the last words we have from the pen of the apostle Paul...The hard-earned lessons of Paul's years of service are concentrated here so that these epistles, brief though they are, contain a priceless spiritual treasure."
Philip C. Johnson

NOTABLE NOTES

Some Bible students believe that Titus may have been the brother of Luke, author of the third Gospel and the book of Acts. Titus left the island of Crete temporarily, as Paul requested (see Titus 3:12), and was sent by the apostle into Dalmatia (see 2 Timothy 4:10). Following that, tradition states that Titus returned to the island of Crete and became the spiritual overseer of the church work, eventually dying there at a good old age.

CHRIST CONNECTIONS

Christ can be found in Titus as:
One Who Appoints the Leaders in the Church
Coming Savior

PHILEMON

AUTHOR: **Paul**

THEME: **Forgiveness**

CATEGORY: **Pauline Epistle**

FASCINATING FACTS

1. Philemon is perhaps Paul's most personal letter and one of his least doctrinal.

2. Philemon is Paul's shortest epistle.

3. Philemon is one of only three individuals to whom Paul wrote; the others were Timothy and Titus.

4. Philemon is Paul's only letter written both to an individual (verse 1), as well as to a family and a church (verse 2).

5. Though a brief letter of only twenty-five verses, Philemon mentions eleven people by name.

6. Philemon is one of Paul's most tactful and discreet pieces of writing in the midst of a very controversial subject (slavery).

7. Philemon is possibly the only letter that Paul may have written for himself without the help of a secretary (verse 19).

8. Paul's letter to Philemon is one of the most beautiful examples in all of Scripture of our forgiveness, reconciliation, and justification in Christ.

9. Philemon is the only New Testament Book to give us an inside peek into the Christian home of that day.

10. Philemon is one of Paul's four prison epistles; the others are Ephesians, Philippians, and Colossians.

QUOTABLE QUOTES

"A masterly lovely example of love...for we are all His Onesimi (forgiven sinners like Onesimus) if we will believe it."
Martin Luther

"This letter is absolutely unique, not only in the Pauline literature, but in all literature."
W. Graham Scroggie

"It is a masterpiece, and a model of graceful, tactful, and delicate pleading."
Robert Lee

"The whole letter is of pure gold. No wonder the church placed it into the canon."
R. C. H. Lenski

"Paul's epistle to Philemon far surpasses all the wisdom of the world."

A. H. Francke

NOTABLE NOTES

It has been estimated that there were as many as six million slaves in the Roman Empire in Paul's day. There were Christian slaveholders like Philemon within the church. The New Testament does not directly address the institution of slavery as such, but instead offered guidelines both for Christian masters and Christian slaves.

CHRIST CONNECTIONS

Christ can be found in Philemon as:
Controller of the Destiny of His Servants

HEBREWS

IMPORTANT INFORMATION

AUTHOR: **Unknown**

THEME: **The Superiority of Christ and Christianity**

CATEGORY: **General Epistle**

FASCINATING FACTS

1. Hebrews is the only New Testament book with an unknown author.

2. Hebrews is the only New Testament book that deals specifically with the present ministry and activities of Jesus Christ as our High Priest.

3. Hebrews has no introductory greeting, as most New Testament letters do.

4. Hebrews is second only to the book of Revelation in its number of quotations from the Old Testament.

5.   More than twenty descriptive phrases are used of Christ in this book ("heir of all things," "High Priest," etc.).

6.   The epistle to the Hebrews, along with 2 Peter and Jude, makes more references to Jewish history than other New Testament books.

7.   Hebrews is the only New Testament book to give us some typological understanding of the Old Testament feasts and offerings found in Leviticus.

8.   Hebrews contains five very serious warnings against turning away from the Lord (2:1–4; 3:7–4:13; 5:11–6:20; 10:26–39; 12:25–29).

9.   Hebrews contains more than 150 Greek words that are unique to this book.

10. Hebrews is considered by many scholars and commentators to be the greatest literary work in the New Testament, written in some of the most elegant Greek of the New Testament.

11. All of the Old Testament quotations in Hebrews are from the Septuagint (Greek) version of the Old Testament, rather than the more common Hebrew version.

QUOTABLE QUOTES

"Only God knows who wrote the book of Hebrews."
Origen

"The book of Hebrews was written to the Hebrews to tell them to stop acting like Hebrews."
Donald Grey Barnhouse

"The Epistle to the Hebrews is one of the great but much neglected treasures of the New Testament."
D. Edmond Hiebert

"We may compare it [Hebrews] to a painting of perfect beauty, which has been regarded as a work of Raphael. If it should be proved that it was not painted by Raphael, we have thereby not lost a classical piece of art, but gained another master of first rank!"
Thiersch

"Hebrews begins like an essay, proceeds like a sermon, and ends like a letter."
T. Rees

NOTABLE NOTES

John Owen, the noted Puritan theologian and preacher, spent sixteen years of his life writing an eight-volume commentary just on the book of Hebrews! And William Gouge, an eighteenth century preacher who pastored one of the largest churches in London for forty-five years, spent thirty-three of those years just preaching on the book of Hebrews!

CHRIST CONNECTIONS

Christ can be found in Hebrews as:
Son and Image of God
Captain and Author of Our Salvation
Apostle and High Priest

JAMES

AUTHOR: James, the Brother of Jesus

THEME: The Practice of the Christian Faith

CATEGORY: General Epistle

FASCINATING FACTS

1. James is probably the earliest of the twenty-seven New Testament books.

2. James was one of the last books to be accepted into the New Testament canon of Scripture.

3. James is one of only two New Testament books written by a brother of Jesus (see also: Jude).

4. The epistle of James has more figures of speech, analogies, and illustrations from nature than all of the apostle Paul's epistles combined.

5. While James does not ever quote Jesus directly, he does present more of Christ's personal teachings than any other New Testament writer.

6. The language of the Sermon on the Mount is reflected more in this epistle than in any other New Testament book.

7. In many ways, James is the "Proverbs" of the New Testament.

8. James begins and ends with the subject of trials.

9. James is the most practical book in the New Testament, containing very little formal theology.

10. The epistle of James is very Jewish in nature (with no mention of Gentile believers), and contains twenty-two allusions to Old Testament books.

QUOTABLE QUOTES

"If God gives you St. Paul's faith, you will soon have St. James' works."
Augustus M. Toplady

"The Epistle of James is not an epistle of straw; rather it is an epistle of strength. It is not destitute of evangelic character but rather characteristic of the evangel."
Lehman Strauss

"Perhaps there was never a time when the testimony of James, rightly understood, had a more necessary application than now."
C. I. Scofield

NOTABLE NOTES

Martin Luther, the leader of the great Protestant Reformation, was not fond of the epistle of James. Luther objected to it on the basis that he felt that it spoke too much about good works and not enough about faith. He also felt that it taught too little about Christ and the gospel. Even though Luther called James "an epistle of straw, and destitute of evangelic character," he nevertheless considered it to be the Word of God, though not one of the chief books.

CHRIST CONNECTIONS

Christ can be found in James as:
Unchangeable Father
Wisdom of God
Husbandman
Coming Lord

1 PETER

AUTHOR: **Peter**

THEME: **Grace in Times of Suffering**

CATEGORY: **General Epistle**

FASCINATING FACTS

1. Peter is one of only three original disciples used by God to write New Testament books or epistles (see also: Matthew and John).

2. The suffering of Christ is spoken of in every chapter of 1 Peter.

3. In 1 Peter, the subject of suffering is mentioned over fifteen times.

4. 1 Peter has been called the "Job" of the New Testament, as it deals with suffering and God's sovereignty.

5. In 1 Peter, there are more Old Testament quotations, proportionately, than in any other New Testament book.

6. Peter is one of only two New Testament authors to refer to Jesus as a "Lamb" in 1 Peter 1:19 (John was the other; see John 1:29, 36 and Revelation 5:6).

7. 1 Peter was probably written in the early stages of the great Christian persecution under Caesar Nero in Rome.

8. In chapter 5, Peter includes a special word of exhortation for the elders of the church, of which he was one (5:1–4).

9. 1 Peter was one of the earliest New Testament books to be accepted as inspired, while 2 Peter was one of the last.

10. In writing his epistles, Peter was fulfilling the command given to him by Jesus to feed, teach, and shepherd God's people (see John 21:15–17).

QUOTABLE QUOTES

"The portrait of Peter in the Gospels and his own writings are amazingly and gloriously different. In the former, Peter saw his Lord transfigured; in the latter, we see Peter transfigured by the boundless grace of God."
Robert Lee

"Of all the writings of the New Testament, the First Epistle of Peter is perhaps the most anciently and most unanimously attested."
Dean Farrar

"1 Peter is a favorite book because of its practical approach to the needs of every believer . . . This little epistle provides a splendid source of peace and comfort for all God's people who are perplexed and troubled."
J. Allen Blair

NOTABLE NOTES

Peter seemed to have an appreciation and fondness for the word "precious." In his two epistles, Peter tells us about seven "precious" things that we either possess or are, by God's grace. In 1 Peter these are: salvation (1:7), Christ's blood (1:19), God's people (2:4), Christ Himself (2:7), and inner Christian beauty (3:4). In 2 Peter these are: our faith (1:1) and God's promises (1:4).

CHRIST CONNECTIONS

Christ can be found in 1 Peter as:
One Who Was Resurrected
Chief Cornerstone

2 PETER

IMPORTANT INFORMATION

AUTHOR: **Peter**

THEME: **Full Knowledge of the Truth**

CATEGORY: **General Epistle**

FASCINATING FACTS

1. The epistle of 2 Peter consists of the apostle's last recorded, written words (1:14).

2. The authorship and canonicity of 2 Peter have been challenged and attacked perhaps more than any other New Testament book.

3. Only 2 Peter and Jude contain New Testament references to the fall of angels (see 2 Peter 2:4; Jude 6).

4. 2 Peter contains one of the two main statements on the inspiration of Scripture, 2 Peter 1:20–21 (see also: 2 Timothy 3:16).

5. 2 Peter is the only New Testament book that describes how the heavens and earth will pass away (3:10–13).

6. Peter is the only New Testament writer to refer to the inspired writings of another New Testament writer, Paul (3:15–16).

7. There are many similarities and parallels between 2 Peter and Jude, and Jude probably borrowed from Peter's writing.

8. After the first verse, Peter always uses the title of "Lord" in every reference to Jesus.

9. In 2 Peter, one entire chapter out of three is devoted to the subject of false teachers (chapter 2).

10. In this second epistle, Peter makes reference to his experience on the Mount of Transfiguration (1:16b–18).

QUOTABLE QUOTES

"Peter is quick to remind us that the believer can and will conquer through conflict. Times may be harsh and corruption rampant, but those whose faith rests in the Lord will not only survive, they will be victorious."
Charles R. Swindoll

"The letter is a strong appeal to Christians to develop a character and conduct consistent with a true faith. As Peter writes, he has his eye on his own approaching death, but even more upon the glorious coming of Christ."
Cary N. Weisiger III

"The best defense is a strong offense. Peter illustrated that axiom by calling his readers to a life of maturity as the best safeguard against the inroads of apostasy."
Robert G. Gromacki

NOTABLE NOTES

Though his death is not recorded in the pages of Scripture, tradition states that Peter was martyred under the cruel hand of the Roman Emperor, Nero. Tradition affirms that Peter was crucified on a cross outside of Rome. However, because Peter did not feel worthy to die in the same manner as his Lord, he requested to be crucified upside-down, and was obliged.

CHRIST CONNECTIONS

Christ can be found in 2 Peter as:
Savior
Coming One
Deliverer

1 JOHN

IMPORTANT INFORMATION

AUTHOR: John the Apostle

THEME: Living in the Light

CATEGORY: General Epistle

FASCINATING FACTS

1. 1 John contains no greeting or opening address.

2. John uses the affectionate term of "little children," in reference to believers, a total of nine times—more than any other New Testament writer.

3. 1 John contains two of the three great "God is" statements that John gave (1:5; 4:16).

4. 1 John contains many contrasts: light and darkness, love and hatred, truth and falsehood, Christ and antichrists, and so on.

5. 1 John contains no quotations from the Old Testament.

6. In 1 John, the word "know" and its equivalent are used more than thirty times (John's refutation of gnosticism: to know).

7. 1 John makes a dozen references to Jesus in this brief epistle, and His name is found in every chapter.

8. 1 John provides one of the most definitive statements on worldliness (2:15–17).

9. 1 John is one of only two books in the Bible to use the term "antichrist" (see also: 2 John).

10. In John's three epistles, the word "truth" is a key word, which is found some twenty times.

QUOTABLE QUOTES

"It is a family letter from the Father to His 'little children' who are in the world. With the possible exception of the Song of Solomon, it is the most intimate of the inspired writings."
C. I. Scofield

"John, who was with the Lord from the very first, is the very last to write. It seems as if he, who knew and loved the Lord so intimately and deeply, is set to guard His glory and the infinite worth of the Person of our blessed Lord, against the fearful departure from the truth of God."
August Van Ryn

"John is saying that Jesus Christ is God's communication to us. Jesus is the noun of God, the verb of God, the adjective of God. Jesus articulates God. When you look at Jesus Christ you see the love of God."
Jerry Vines

NOTABLE NOTES

John was an elderly man in the vicinity of ninety years of age when he wrote his final letters. As far as we know, he is the only one of the original disciples to die of old age and of natural causes. Tradition states that the Roman Emperor, Domitian, had John condemned to boil in a cauldron of oil, but God supernaturally protected John, and he emerged unharmed. After being banished to the Island of Patmos for a period of time, John eventually returned to Ephesus, where he is believed to have died at a good old age.

CHRIST CONNECTIONS

Christ can be found in 1 John as:

Word of Life

Advocate

Propitiator

Messiah

2 JOHN

IMPORTANT INFORMATION

AUTHOR: John the Apostle

THEME: Walking in Truth

CATEGORY: General Epistle

FASCINATING FACTS

1. 2 John is the second shortest book in the Bible (see also: 3 John).

2. 2 John is one of only three personal letters in the New Testament (see also: 3 John, Philemon).

3. 2 John is the only book in the Bible addressed to a woman—if the "Elect Lady" is not a reference to a church (1:1).

4. 2 John is one of only two books in the Bible to use the term "antichrist" (1 John).

5. In 2 John, the word "truth" is a key word and is found five times and some twenty times in John's three epistles combined.

6. 2 John was one of the last books to be accepted into the New Testament canon of Scripture.

7. In 2 John, the author does not identify either himself or his recipients outright (1:1).

8. Of the thirteen verses in 2 John, at least eight of them are found directly or indirectly in 1 John.

9. 2 and 3 John are the only two New Testament books addressed from "The Elder."

10. In 2 John, we have John's stern warning that false teachers are not to be invited into our homes, or even to be bid Godspeed (verses 10–11).

QUOTABLE QUOTES

"The Second Epistle of John may be the most neglected book in the New Testament."
Jerry Vines

"Though he understood and interpreted the person and work of Jesus more intimately than any other writer in the New Testament, and though he was in a life and death struggle with evil, he took time to pen this little personal note to one Christian woman, bringing joy to her heart and strengthening her in her own battle with evil forces which swirled about her."
Herschel H. Hobbs

"Here in the Second Epistle, truth is insisted on. We are shown that love must be in the truth, and does not go beyond the bounds which truth imposes."
August Van Ryn

NOTABLE NOTES

An old tradition states that the "Elect Lady" addressed here in 2 John is Martha, the good friend of Jesus. One scholar suggests that the Greek word for "lady" (kuria), is "Martha" in Hebrew. If this tradition about Martha is true, then the "elect sister," mentioned in verse 13, would be Martha's sister Mary.

CHRIST CONNECTIONS

Christ can be found in 2 John as:
Son of God
God Come in the Flesh

3 JOHN

AUTHOR: **John the Apostle**

THEME: **Hospitality**

CATEGORY: **General Epistle**

FASCINATING FACTS

1. 3 John is the shortest book in the Bible.

2. 3 John is one of only three personal letters in the New Testament (see also: 2 John, Philemon).

3. 3 John contains one of the briefest New Testament greetings.

4. 3 John is the only book in the Bible dedicated entirely to the subject of hospitality.

5. 3 John is the only New Testament book in which the names "Jesus" or "Christ" do not appear.

6. 3 John is written with great affection (1:1, 2, 5, 11).

7. In 3 John, the word "truth" is a key word and is found six times and some twenty times John's three epistles combined.

8. John's first epistle was written to believers; his second epistle to a woman; and this third epistle to a man.

9. 3 and 2 John are the only two New Testament books addressed from "The Elder."

10. Gaius, to whom this letter is addressed, was probably not one of the three well-known associates of Paul, since this Gaius was evidently converted under John's ministry (verse 4).

QUOTABLE QUOTES

"My old teacher, A. T. Robertson, was fond of telling us that when we were in the pastorate we must love the people, 'warts and all'...It is against such a background that we can best understand 3 John."
Herschel H. Hobbs

"When truth and love come into conflict, truth must always survive."
J. Vernon McGee

"This little letter gives us a glimpse into an early assembly, its people and its problems. As you read this brief letter, you find yourself saying, 'Times have not changed very much!' We have similar people and problems today!"
Warren W. Wiersbe

NOTABLE NOTES

In the early days of Christianity, many of the evangelists were called to an itinerant ministry. This meant that they were dependent upon kind and generous believers like Gaius (verse 6) to open their homes and to provide their basic necessities, such as a hot meal and a place to sleep. These evangelists would take nothing from the unsaved (verse 7) lest they appeared to be peddling the gospel.

CHRIST CONNECTIONS

Christ can be found in 3 John as:
Truth
One Who Is Good

JUDE

IMPORTANT INFORMATION

AUTHOR: **Jude**

THEME: **Contending for the Faith**

CATEGORY: **General Epistle**

FASCINATING FACTS

1. Jude is one of only two New Testament books written by a brother of Jesus (see also: James).

2. Jude is the only book in the Bible solely devoted to the subject of apostasy.

3. Jude has more non-canonical references (three) than any other New Testament book (verse 9, the Assumption of Moses; verses 6, 14–15, the book of Enoch).

4. The book of Jude, along with Hebrews and 2 Peter, makes more references to Jewish history than other New Testament books.

5. There are approximately a dozen groups of triads in this brief epistle (verse 1: called, sanctified, and preserved; verse 8: defile, reject, and speak evil; and so on.).

6. Jude addresses the most general audience of all the New Testament epistles (verse 1).

7. Only Jude and 2 Peter contain Scripture references to fallen angels being chained (Jude verse 6; 2 Peter 2:4).

8. Only in the epistle of Jude is Michael referred to as an archangel (verse 9). No other archangels are mentioned as such in Scripture.

9. Jude's epistle is very similar in content and theme to 2 Peter 2, and he apparently continued the previous warnings of Peter (verses 17–18).

10. In many ways, Jude is the "Book of Judges" of the New Testament.

11. Jude has often been referred to as "The Acts of the Apostates."

12. Jude is the only book of the Bible to reference Michael and Satan disputing over the body of Moses.

QUOTABLE QUOTES

Studying the little book of Jude is like working a gold mine because of all the rich nuggets which are here just for the mining."
J. Vernon McGee

"Jude is the only book in all of God's Word entirely devoted to the great apostasy which is to come upon Christendom before the Lord Jesus Christ returns. Without Jude, the prophetic picture which begins with the teachings of Christ in the Gospels and develops throughout the epistles would be incomplete."
S. Maxwell Coder

"A clash of cymbals! A boom of tympani! A cannon blast and a cascade of fireworks! That is what the letter of Jude is like. The words of this apostle thunder from the pages."
Ray C. Stedman

NOTABLE NOTES

Even though the early church father Jerome considered the epistle of Jude to be a part of the New Testament Scriptures, he still regarded it as a disputed book. His reasoning stemmed from the fact that Jude alludes to non-biblical sources—those being 1 Enoch and the Assumption of Moses.

CHRIST CONNECTIONS

Christ can be found in Jude as:
Preserver
Coming Judge
Merciful One

REVELATION

IMPORTANT INFORMATION

AUTHOR: **John the Apostle**

THEME: **The Revelation of Jesus Christ for the Last Days**

CATEGORY: **Prophecy**

FASCINATING FACTS

1. Revelation is the only New Testament book that focuses primarily on prophetic and future events.

2. Revelation is the only book of the Bible that pronounces a special blessing for reading, hearing, and obeying the prophecy within (1:3).

3. Revelation pronounces a distinct curse at the end (22:18–19).

4. Revelation contains more symbolism than any other New Testament book.

5. Revelation begins and ends with the Second Coming of Christ.

6. Revelation is the only book in Scripture that refers to the "thousand years" (Millennium) specifically by name (20:2, 3, 4, 5, 6, 7).

7. Revelation contains more references to, and more quotations from, the Old Testament than any other book in the New Testament.

8. In the book of Revelation, Jesus is referred to as the "Lamb" some twenty-eight times.

9. Revelation contains more references to numbers, especially seven (more than fifty times) and twelve (over twenty times), than any other New Testament book.

10. Revelation ends much of what Genesis began: the curse of mankind, death, sorrow, tears, and so on.

11. Revelation is the only New Testament book written that is based upon a vision (1:10).

12. Revelation is the last book written in the Bible, chronologically (approximately A.D. 95).

13. Revelation contains John's final, recorded written words.

14. Revelation gives more titles for the Savior than any other book in the Bible.

15. Revelation records the name of Satan more than any other New Testament book (seven times).

16. Revelation is the only book in the Bible that gives its own natural outline (1:19).

17. Revelation is one of the few books of the Bible to contain its own title (1:1).

18. Revelation is the only one of the five New Testament books written by John in which he identifies himself by name (1:1, 4, 9; 21:2; 22:8).

19. Revelation is one of the few books in the Bible to state the exact location of its writing (1:9).

20. In Revelation, the ministry of angels is very prominent, and angels are mentioned some seventy-four times.

21. John is one of only two biblical figures commanded by God to eat a scroll (see also: Ezekiel).

QUOTABLE QUOTES

"I do not understand all the details of the book of Revelation but there is a special blessing promised to all who read, hear, and keep its message and I don't want to miss that blessing."
Vance Havner

"The book of Revelation is a source of happiness to anyone who will read it, hear it in the depths of his heart, and obey its instructions. If ever a generation needed to study this book, it is ours. We are probably living at the time when these things will begin to come to pass."
Tim LaHaye

"The book of Revelation has suffered an unfortunate fate. On the whole either it has been abandoned by the readers of the Bible as being almost completely unintelligible, or it has become the happy hunting ground of religious eccentrics, who seek to construct from it a kind of celestial timetable of events to come."
William Barclay

NOTABLE NOTES

There are four separate earthquakes foretold in Revelation: at the opening of the sixth seal (6:12), at the opening of the seventh seal (8:5), at the raising of the two witnesses (11:13), and at the pouring out of the seventh vial at Armageddon (16:16–21).

CHRIST CONNECTIONS

Christ can be found in Revelation as:
Coming One
Beginning and End
Son of Man
Great Judge
Lion of Judah
Conquering One
Lamb
Bridegroom
Faithful and True
Word of God

BIBLIOGRAPHY

THE MACARTHUR STUDY BIBLE . . . . JOHN F. MACARTHUR JR.

THE RYRIE STUDY BIBLE . . . . CHARLES C. RYRIE

THE NIV STUDY BIBLE . . . . KENNETH BARKER, GEN. ED.

BE SKILLFUL . . . . WARREN W. WIERSBE

BE HOLY . . . . WARREN W. WIERSBE

BE STRONG . . . . WARREN W. WIERSBE

BE COMMITTED . . . . WARREN W. WIERSBE

TALK THRU THE BIBLE . . . . WILKINSON/BOA

WILLMINGTON'S BIBLE HANDBOOK . . . . H. L. WILLMINGTON

WILLMINGTON'S GUIDE TO THE BIBLE . . . . H. L. WILLMINGTON

WILLMINGTON'S SURVEY OF THE OLD TESTAMENT . . . . H. L. WILLMINGTON

PICTORIAL INTRODUCTION TO THE BIBLE . . . . WILLIAM S. DEAL

PREACHING THROUGH THE BIBLE . . . . ERIC W. HAYDEN

THE OUTLINED BIBLE . . . . ROBERT LEE

KNOW YOUR BIBLE . . . . W. GRAHAM SCROGGIE

EXPLORE THE BOOK . . . . J. SIDLOW BAXTER

THE ANNOTATED BIBLE . . . . ARNO C. GAEBELEIN

ZONDERVAN'S PICTORIAL BIBLE DICTIONARY . . . . MERRILL C. TENNEY

WHAT THE BIBLE IS ALL ABOUT . . . . D. HENRIETTA C. MEARS

THE BIBLE BOOK BY BOOK . . . . G. COLEMAN LUCK

NELSON'S ILLUSTRATED BIBLE DICTIONARY . . . . HERBERT LOCKYER SR., GEN. ED.

THE NEW UNGER'S BIBLE DICTIONARY . . . . MERRILL F. UNGER

THE NEW TESTAMENT SURVEY . . . . ROBERT G. GROMACKI

AN INTRODUCTION TO THE NEW TESTAMENT, VOLS. 1-3 . . . . D. EDMOND HEIBERT

NEW TESTAMENT INTRODUCTION, VOLS. 1-3 . . . . DONALD GUTHRIE

Information in the "Christ Connections" sections adapted from: http://
www.free-bible-study-lessons.com/Christ-in-the-Bible.html

ABOUT THE AUTHOR

Jeff Lasseigne is the Assistant Pastor at Harvest Christian Fellowship in Riverside, California. Since coming on staff in 1989, his primary responsibilities have included ongoing Bible teaching, church administration, and leadership training.

Jeff and his wife, Lorraine, have three adult children and six grandchildren. They make their home in Riverside.